VALUE-DRIVEN

The CIO's Handbook for Digital Transformation and Innovation in the Public Sector

D. Brent Messer

Tripel  Press

Tripel Press, LLC.
1001 S. Main St., STE 500
Kalispell , MT 59901
info@tripelpress.com   www.tripelpress.com

Printed in the United States of America, La Vergne, Tennessee.

First Edition
25 24 23 22 21 | 10 9 8 7 6 5 4 3 2 1

ISBN: 978-1-7369364-0-5
Library of Congress Control Number: 2021936490

Companion Website
For updates, errata, and free copies of the diagrams, charts, and worksheets discussed in this book, visit the companion website at www.valuedrivenbook.com

Tripel Press books are printed on long-lasting acid-free paper that has been manufactured through environmentally sustainable and responsable processes when possible.

Produced, designed, indexed, and cover design by 423 Media. (www.423media.com); copyedited and proofed by Matthew McDarmont; set in Adobe Garamond Pro.

To all the great innovators dedicated to public service, may you all be successful in your efforts to champion and enable change.

CONTENTS

FOREWORD

For the better part of two decades, I have dedicated my professional life to supporting, educating, challenging, and cheering on public sector technology professionals, with a particular focus on Chief Information Officers, as a faculty member at the University of North Carolina at Chapel Hill's School of Government. During this time, I have been fortunate enough to meet and work alongside some of the most talented, most dedicated IT professionals across the United States who epitomize the concept of servant leadership. These public sector CIOs hail from all sizes and types of government entities, but they all operate under a guiding ethos of service to the community through excellence in technology solution provision. Brent Messer is one of those I have been fortunate enough to know for the majority of my career, and I have witnessed his professional growth through the ranks of the classic IT career progression to become one of the foremost thought leaders within the public sector CIO realm. Brent has created this book as a labor of love to help guide other CIOs and those who seek to grow into that role in the most critical aspects of CIO leadership and innovation.

When Brent shared his book idea with me, I was immediately enthusiastic about how much value his content could create, not just for our public sector CIOs, but for our governments, our residents, and our communities. While the public sector has made incredible strides in technology investments over the past several decades, those investments have been centered on internal, operational efficiencies. Brent and other leading-edge CIOs have pushed their public sector entities to move beyond the status quo and leverage technology not only as a means of delivering more efficient and effective services, but also to help the entity gain and maintain a competitive economic development advantage.

In this book, Brent shares his valuable insight on how public sector CIOs can use strategic value-based leadership to further innovate, inspire, and exceed expectations. The book offers key insights on critical topics such as leadership, governance, culture management, and performance management to often-neglected topics of agility and innovation. Without a doubt, Brent Messer has created an excellent field guide to help prepare the reader for excellence as a public sector CIO.

Shannon H. Tufts, PhD

INTRODUCTION

I want to cover something important, right up front. A mindset that every CIO should have, and it is something I am constantly telling members of my organization including my staff. We in IT have one single product we produce that helps drive the organization forward. When focused on by the IT group, this single product can displace old technologies and drive innovation. That product is not email; It is not a network, technology consulting, help desk service, telecommunications, network redundancy, information assurance, nor any other IT services terms you hear among the IT groups. So then what is that one product that IT in any organization, in any field—especially the public sector—provides? Right now, as I write this, I can suddenly hear the loud comedic voice of my colleague Robb yelling from the back of the audience with a Tennessee drawl… "VAL-UE!" And he's right. The CIO and IT Group's primary objective in any organization is to strategically use technology to transform and innovate, providing VALUE. Yes, we provide connectivity as well as communications and various other services and systems, but strategically combined, they should all offer a significant and tangible value.

At the beginning of technology entering the public sector, the IT groups of organizations were primarily a support function that provided expertise specifically in finance information systems—the first information systems to be added to almost all organizations. Eventually, IT evolved beyond just single expert systems to maintaining several systems across the entire organization. However, IT was usually just an afterthought. A necessary cost center to help keep a competitive advantage in the market—or in the case of government, just get them up to speed and keep up with the times. This was pretty much the norm for IT from the late 1960s until as recently as 2003. The U.S. Army has a term for these operations that was befitting at that time; "In the rear with the gear." Behind closed doors in backrooms and basements worldwide, the geeky IT experts silently program and maintain mainframes, dummy terminals, tape drives, and other such systems that some front-line workers use in daily operations to help generate revenue or provide more efficient services for constituents.

Back when programming a computer just meant feeding it instructions to generate reports, search through data, or compute calculations—where the term computer came from in the first place. It wasn't even called IT; it was mostly called data processing.

Over the last fifty-plus years, the role of the person in charge of these back-office IT operations has also evolved. Titles changed, from Lead Computer Operator to Manager or Director of Data Processing, Director of Information Technology, and eventually to Chief Information Officer. In the early to mid-2000s, the CIO's role began to morph into less of a technical role and more of an executive role. This also applies to the title Director of IT, which is somewhat synonymous with CIO in some local governments and smaller private sector firms. CIO's began focusing on having excellent business acumen and understanding the market of their organization more so than the technical aspects of configuring switches and routers or engineering software, regardless of if that was their educational background. CIOs needed a seat at the executive table to do their jobs effectively and add value to the organization instead of just being a back-office cost center. But in the early days of the CIO role—and unfortunately still today in some government agencies—that wasn't happening, and CIO's had to figure out how to read minds to add value. Of course, the private sector picked up on this first. The private sector conceived the CIO's title when most government agencies still used titles from the '80s and '90s to describe their head of IT. Most government agencies back then were several years behind the curve—some still are. Somewhere around 2005, most government organizations began adopting the title of CIO but still didn't entirely embrace the true meaning of the role and how it fits into the organization. Like with anything in government, as more and more government agencies, cities, counties, and states began adopting the title of CIO as their "chief of all computer-related matters," slowly the role started to change again to follow the private sector's usual head start. I wish I could say that finally, all government organizations have come around to the concept of giving the CIO a seat at the executive table. However, as of the date I wrote this, that is unfortunately still not the case.

Government CIOs must indeed have a seat at the executive leadership table. Their role is no longer that of back-office technology manager, maintainer, and preverbal geek. Today, the CIO is a strategic partner in any organization's success, especially government organizations, where things can be incredibly complex. And it's not about whom the CIO directly reports to as long as the communication lines are open and well received. As the CIO for the City of Chattanooga, I was very fortunate that I had a seat at the table from day one on the job and did not have to fight for it. I was a trusted member of the executive team, which made my job a whole lot easier. Hopefully, you, and many others like you who are striving to become public sector CIOs, will have a similar experience when you first move into the role as a CIO. However, I am sure some of you are in for a real struggle.

I wrote this book primarily as a teaching tool for those in the public sector IT field who aspire to one day become a government CIO. Still, it is just as useful for current government CIOs and other government executives alike. IT adding value and finding ways to innovate in government is a concept that is unfortunately somewhat rare in the public sector. I hope this book can help bridge that gap in government organizations worldwide.

THE TERMINOLOGY USED IN THIS BOOK

Before we move on, I want to clarify some of the terminologies I use in this book. While different organizations in both the private and public sectors use similar terms to describe how they are organized, there are just too many nuances to assume every reader—regardless of where they live in the world—will be on the same page and using the same vernacular. Therefore, I have highlighted a few terms that I use throughout the book. I use the general term Chief Executive to mean Mayor, City or County Manager, Bureau Chief, Bureau Director, CEO, Minister, or any other title referring to an organization's top executive. When referring to the senior-most executive leader of Information Technology (e.g. CIO, CTO, Director of IT, etc.), I use the title CIO. And, finally, while some agencies refer to this field as Information Services or IS—not synonymous with IS meaning Information Systems—I will refer to the general area of practice as only IT or Information Technology.

DEPARTMENT OR DIVISION OR OTHER?

In some organizations, the division is the highest organizational divide, followed by departments, sections, teams, etc. In a lot of the local government agencies, it is department first, then division, etc. This book uses the general term IT Group to mean all IT components as a group, department, division, team, whatever it is. I am also assuming that the IT group reports directly to the CIO. You may have a different organizational structure, which is okay; the principles in this book will ultimately be the same.

COMPANION WEBSITE

For more information about the topics in this book and free copies of the diagrams, charts, and worksheets discussed in this book, visit the companion website at http://valuedrivenbook.com

PART ONE
LEADERSHIP

CHAPTER ONE
LEAD FROM THE FRONT

"If your actions inspire others to dream more, learn more, do more, and become more, you are a leader."
~ John Quincy Adams

The first step in creating any value to your organization as a CIO is to be a good leader. Leadership in this role is not an option. So, I want to start by discussing the differences between a good leader and a poor leader. Many people think they know what leadership is, especially managers and up. However, it should come as no surprise, some are incorrect. I travel internationally to speak at various events. And at these events, I have had private and social conversations with many government CIOs and other government IT staff. I have also talked to CIOs, and IT staff doing research for this book. Let me tell you, there are a few more leadership poor government CIOs out there than you would think.

When I go to conferences, I make it a point to sit next to attendees I don't know at every session or during meals. A technique I learned from my friend and colleague Jonathan Feldman, the CIO for the City of Asheville, NC. It's good to meet new people, and the conversations are usually excellent. The ideas I get speaking to people from all walks of life in this industry are inspirational. However, I occasionally find some individuals who are… well shall we say, somewhat frustrating to converse with. A few years ago, one fellow I met at a public sector CIO conference in Bethesda, Maryland, had some charming points of view. I asked him some questions about some of my research for this book, explained its concept and where I was going with it. I was flabbergasted when he said I should "just stick to the new technology and technology implementation methods, not leadership…" [because] "that's where the value truly is." His justification was that "leadership is an easy skill that you must already know to get the CIO job in the first place. Why else would you have been hired." It was an excruciating conversation which would have almost assuredly turned into a heated debate had it not thankfully been interrupted by the after-dinner cocktails.

Unfortunately, this is not an uncommon thought among many government leaders in general, much less CIOs. I personally have experienced working for a government CIO like that firsthand. He also had misconceptions of his role, including delusions of grandeur and a false sense of his "superior" leadership abilities. Perhaps you, too, have worked for, or maybe still work for a CIO like this. If so, please don't use that as an example of how to lead. Please understand that you don't have to be an all-knowing and wise leader to lead an IT group or anyone else for that matter. However, you do have to be honest and self-aware and continuously learning how to be a better leader—just one of many ingredients that makes a great leader.

For now, as a means to reiterate these concepts, I want to introduce you to an entirely made-up CIO, called Fred. The scenarios I will describe are authentic and were literally said or done by several actual government CIOs who worked for some government agency, or agencies, somewhere in the good ol' US of A. If you know any CIO who coincidently happens to be called Fred, and he too has done these things, I swear I wasn't using him as an example—pure coincidence. But hey, if the shoe fits!

What you are about to read in the coming chapter really does happen and has a significant negative impact on the organization as a whole. The morale of the IT staff working for Fred and these actions even support the old assumption that government employees are lazy, uneducated, and undedicated to doing a good job. You know what I mean, one government worker digging while five others stand around the hole and supervise. Or, the old joke about the new Mayor. Being introduced to the senior staff, who are all standing around with their heads up their rear-ends, except one guy in the corner standing upright sipping coffee. Then the Mayor asks, "what's with that guy?" The supervisor showing the Mayor around replies, "Oh, he's new." Yeah, that! I'm sure you have heard them all before. Well, I can tell you it's not always the staff that is the issue. It can also be the poor leadership skills of supervisors on up to executives in the public sector, driving that misconception home.

Fred is one of those CIOs that think management and leadership are the same things. Management and leadership are not synonymous, here are some quick and easy definitions to differentiate the two.

Management really is about the control and monitoring of processes and work in an organization. Managers are concerned about productivity, not strategy.

Leadership is the ability to influence people to follow your lead and direction. Basically leading people vs. managing work.

Since we are boiling all this down to value, it really comes down to managers count value while leaders create value.

So, Fred spends his time as the CIO for his organization micromanaging every detailed process, project, and person. To Fred, that is leadership. Now, Fred wasn't hired directly to be the CIO. Instead, he started back in the early to mid-'90s at the tail end of the "overseers of financial systems" days, and, over the years, grew up with the role changing around him. Not an uncommon thing in local government over the last 40 years, but it is changing now as these folks retire. Eventually, after many years and many title changes, Fred was put in the CIO role.

In organizations that train, mentor, provide education, and pathways for advancement, like the Toyota Motor Corporation, the organization ends up with well-rounded executives who are good, if not great, leaders. On the other hand, Fred was given more and more power over the years but without formal education, training, mentoring, or understanding of how his role was changing. This quickly pushed Fred outside of his expertise and capabilities. However, Fred liked the power and authority he was given. He wore the CIO title well, at least in his opinion.

This is where things start to go awry for Fred, and he doesn't even notice. This scenario, where it spans decades, can be awful for those who don't change with the times because the management paradigms have shifted significantly over the last 40 years. As a result, Fred's IT group is in a constant state of flux with high turnover rates and very low staff morale. Performance suffers and value to the organization is practically non-existent. In Fred's case, his IT group's operations are secluded behind an iron curtain reminiscent of the Cold War days of communist East Germany. Like the citizens of East Germany longed to escape to the free West, so too Fred's staff long to flee from Fred's poor leadership and skip off to IT nirvana.

For Fred, nearly every mistake or mishap that ever occurs under his watch ultimately points back to him—A lack of leadership, direction, and vision on Fred's part and a lack of expertise in the staff he hired. You see, Fred doesn't want to hire anyone he perceives to be smarter than he is. Also, Fred really doesn't understand the skills staff needs to perform their roles effectively. Moreover, when there is turnover, Fred fills the vacancy blindly with the same type of person and skill set he previously had without looking to a future state and determining and potential changes in those roles. For Fred, the mistakes actually seen as mistakes are always shoved under the rug, hidden from the Chief Executive's view. The only thing Fred really reports up the chain to his bosses is the items checked off Fred's master to-do list of organizational requests and projects. Coincidentally, Fred considers this his strategic plan.

Everything produced within Fred's IT group is micromanaged to a ridiculously unrealistic and inefficient degree. It takes longer to report time on a task than to actually complete the task. Even worse, there is no indication of real structure or collaboration within Fred's IT group either. It is pure chaos. Fred's only real concern is making his boss happy. On many occasions, Fred lets his staff know when things don't go as he thinks they should and does so very publicly. If you work for someone like Fred, then I truly am sorry. I wish I had some tremendously wise advice on how to change your boss's ways; but that is simply not realistic; and it's best if you come to grips with that.

Fred is not a leader. Fred is a power-hungry grandiloquent bully who blames others for his misconduct. CIOs like Fred respond to potential outside threats with bully tactics and attempt to thwart and squash any resistance, much like a totalitarian dictator would. This poor leadership behavior also isn't isolated to the Baby Boomer generation, who, like Fred, evolved into the CIO's role from other roles. I have seen just as poor leadership skills in Gen-X'ers and Millennials. While some people are born with an innate ability to lead groups of people toward common objectives, leadership is a soft skill that can be learned through investment of time, education, and desire to do so. If you need a more clear example of what this type of arrogance and complacency will get you, just look back to January 28, 1986 when the space shuttle Challenger exploded over the coast of Florida. A lesson in poor leadership and communication that cost the lives of seven American astronauts and has been taught ever since as an example of what not to do.

I wish I could say that Fred's particular situations were wholly made up just to make a point for this book. I wish I could say that it is a rare and inaccurate description of some IT groups. But unfortunately, it's not. I have come across several CIOs and other executives and managers who ran their area of responsibility and direct reports this way. As one example, take this real-life case in Suffolk, Virginia,[1] where the IT staff finally had enough of their CIO's poor leadership. A coup d'etat took place, which isn't good for either side in the long run. Everyone from the Deputy CIO down took their complaints to the top in hopes of fixing the problems they all faced. That situation eventually led to an efficiency evaluation and audit of the IT group's capability and functionality. The result was a scathing report pointing directly to the CIO as the single most cause of the department's problems. That CIO was relieved of his duties and eventually replaced. The IT Group was drastically restructured, and in the end, the IT staff didn't come out of the situation well either.

The level of segregated and barely supported systems scattered throughout public sector organizations with CIOs who lead like this is almost unfathomable. In several examples I came across, the organization's damage was so significant that it was expected to take several years and untold millions of dollars to repair the neglected IT infrastructure. In one example, the estimated cost to taxpayers to hire the efficiency consultant, replace the CIO, restructure the IT department, replace lost staff, and retrain or weed out the lousy staff and managers hired by the CIO, and then fix the damage to the systems and infrastructure losses, was measured in tens of millions of dollars. All the while, this organization was at serious risk of a ransom ware attack. The biggest shame of situations like these is the damage done to the excellent staff who are talented, hardworking, and dedicated to public service. The staff that looks for mentors to guide them as the next generation of leaders end up getting a lesson in how not to run IT effectively and how not to be a good leader and manager instead of what you should do for true success. Where these poor leadership CIOs go unchecked, their less-experienced subordinates may even take it to mean that it is the appropriate way to lead. And thus, the cycle could continue. Meanwhile, there are always IT staff smart enough to see the situation for face value is where the turnover comes into play. They move on wherever and however they can. Looking for a better environment to work in, and they should.

The impact these poor leaders have on organizations goes beyond segregated and deteriorating IT systems. Studies[2] have shown that crappy bosses don't just make employees unhappy; they make employees unhealthy too. Employees of bad managers are 30% more likely to suffer coronary heart disease. On average, it takes 22 months for an employee to shake off the stress and anxiety caused by a bad boss. This is a colossal waste of potential productivity, not to mention the physiological damage to the employees. In a study published by the Harvard Business Review,[3] the top ten flaws of bad leaders were identified as the following:

1. Fails to inspire.
2. Accepts mediocrity.
3. Lacks clear vision and direction.
4. Unable to collaborate and be a team player.
5. Fails to walk the talk.
6. Failure to improve and learn from mistakes.
7. An inability to lead change or innovate owing resistance to new ideas.
8. A failure to develop others.
9. Inept interpersonal skills.
10. Displays of bad judgment that lead to poor decisions.

When it comes to public sector CIOs specifically, the staff I interviewed from various local government agencies confirm that while those are spot on, the lack of clear vision or direction comes in as the number one flaw. Followed by the failure to inspire staff.

Many people coming into supervisory roles for the first time can easily make these mistakes. I recall when coming out of the U. S. Army and back into civilian life, my idea of good supervisory skills was I say jump; and you say how high. Of course, that was the '90s. Today most branches of the military spend more time and effort to train commissioned and non-commissioned officers in good leadership and motivational skills. That's why it is imperative as an excellent leader to mentor staff, new supervisors, and managers, so they learn the proper way to be a leader. This has another impact I will share later in the next chapter.

Always lead from the front and show them the way. Set the example and mentor as much as possible. Great leaders also have a clear and open understanding of their own strengths and weaknesses and aren't afraid to be viewed as human beings who make mistakes. Poor leaders, like Fred, try to hide their shortcomings and want their peers' perception to be that they don't make any or very few mistakes. Great leaders will openly communicate about what they know and, more importantly, what they don't know. They will also share information through appropriate channels and learn when to leave the details to someone else and trust that person to get the job done.

CHAPTER TWO
BUILD A GREAT CULTURE

❝ *The best way to find out if you can trust somebody is to trust them." ~Ernest Hemingway*

It should not come as a surprise to you that your IT staff will be inherently non-trusting of management or leadership. Why do you suppose that is? Well, just look back to chapter one at Fred and his leadership style to answer that question. As a leader, you must trust the people who work for you. If you don't trust the people who work for you, either you have a problem or you hired the wrong people and need to take different management/performance measures.

Let's assume you are newly moving into the role of CIO. A freshly minted IT executive. In reality, when you move into a CIO role, you will absolutely be inheriting staff you didn't vet or hire yourself or through your subordinate managers. This is the same if you move up through the same organization's ranks—which is rare but not unheard of these days. More likely, you were hired from outside into the organization to take over the role of CIO. Either way, you are inheriting staff someone else hired. If you have never held a position with this much power and responsibility, this high up the chain as CIO before, the first thing to do is, BREATH! I know it's exciting; don't say it isn't, or you are a liar!

The second thing is to calm down and focus. Don't let the excitement—or power—go to your head. Remember, the staff you are taking over are human beings just like you and are in similar positions you were once in. Think back to what that was like. Especially if you have ever been in a situation from the opposite side. A new CIO was coming in when you were the X manager or X of whatever. That's how they feel right now with you coming in. And guess what? They don't trust you! In fact, they are most likely scared of you. For the Freds out there, I would imagine that is a good feeling—people being scared of you. Seriously, don't be a Fred. Nobody wants to work for a Fred.

Okay, so you have just taken over as CIO for X City, County, or State, and inherited X number of staff who are now looking to you for vision and guidance. To that, I say, trust them until you can't trust them. I know that sounds strange, but hear me out. In these cases, I tend to reference Winston Churchill with *"trust, but verify."* In the beginning, the idea is to gain their confidence in you and build your faith in them. To do this you need to jump in headfirst and just trust them. They are going to be on their best behavior. They are going to try to impress you. It's human nature, however, keep in mind that it may also be very stressful for them. They are full of questions and worries, which is typical for any kind of transition.

Here is where it gets time-consuming and sometimes tricky. Now is where you lay out your initial introduction and plans to meet with staff, as well as, how you will spend some time getting to understand the current processes and methods of the IT group you have just inherited. Be extremely observant the first few weeks or so. Take it all in and get the lay of the land. We will do a full assessment on paper later, but for now, just observe. Let staff and the organization go about their usual routine. This will allow the team time to relax and recover from the initial shock of new leadership, not to mention time for you to assess the strengths and weaknesses in the operations and staff.

Depending on the number of staff you have, you may want to consider spending the first few weeks getting to know your employees. This can be done in informal conversations by the proverbial water cooler, or more formally, by setting one-on-one meetings with each of your staff, sometimes taking several weeks or months, depending on the number of staff. This isn't a mandatory task but a helpful one in assessing the current operations and starting down the road to building trust. If you have more than 100 employees then it may not be very practical to meet with all the staff, especially in the 200 and up range. In these cases focus on your managers, directors, and deputies first (i.e. your IT group leadership).

Again, keep in mind this could be scary or even intimidating to some; so be friendly and don't sit across your desk from them.

Don't stand over them. Instead, sit next to or adjacent at a table if you must, however, sometimes it's more comforting with no tables or objects between you and the employee if possible. It's all about perceptions and body language right now. For example, the very presence of you on one side of a big executive desk and your employee on the other sends the message to your employee you are in charge and you know it! This can make them feel inferior, and they may perceive your actions as that. That is not what you want right now. You want to build trust and a professional relationship you can grow on. You want your staff to follow your lead and help fulfill the mission and objectives.

I am six foot four inches tall, quite a large and intimidating person to some. As a result, if possible, when first conversing with staff, I make it a point to try and sit so as to not tower over them in a possibly perceived intimidating manner. President Lyndon B. Johnson used his large frame to do precisely that—intimidate by hovering and leaning over people. This comes in handy in certain situations, but not here and not now.

Crossing arms is also a no-no. It sends the message that you are not interested or closed off. Keep your hands in your lap. Talk with your hands or gesture sure but never crossed or in your pockets. The same applies with leaning back vs. sitting upright or leaning forward. Leaning back too relaxed sends the message you are not really that interested. Leaning forward sends the message that you are intently listening. Also, put your phone down. I met one of my new bosses once, and the entire conversation, he was on his phone texting, only catching every other word I was saying, nodding his head, and just saying "uh-huh." It felt like he didn't care to take the time to listen to my answer to his questions, or care for my opinion on the topic at hand. At least he admitted to me he knew it was a bad habit he needed to address. In the end, he turned out to be a good boss and a good leader.

I know you are busy and sometimes you can't avoid having to text or take a call. Do the right thing, excuse yourself and step out if you really truly must take a call or reply to a text. At the very least, say what you are doing and explain that it's critical communication. Also, be sure to apologize when you are finished. Yes, you heard me correctly. I said apologize. It's common courtesy. Don't just hold up your finger as if to say, "you need to wait!" Do your thing and jump back into the conversation. If you want them to follow you into whatever and wherever, you need them to trust and respect you, which starts with trusting and respecting them.

HIRING THE BEST

Even after you have established yourself and know your staff, you will have to hire at some point. To build a great culture, you must hire only the best and brightest you can find. Former U.S. Secretary of Defense Donald Rumsfeld once said that "[A] people, hire [A] people, and [B] people hire [C] people." Thus we can safely infer that [C] people hire real duds! Always surround yourself with the smartest people you can find. Mentor them and show them how they will in-turn hire the best people, and so on down the line. This is a critical step to building a great culture where staff can thrive and innovate.

With the [A] people concept in mind, here's a fascinating and true story of how this comes into play. I was consulting as part of a hiring committee to hire a higher-level IT Manager in another municipality some time ago. The hiring CIO was pushing out viable candidates because they were "overqualified for the position." In my professional opinion, these candidates were the very cream of the crop, precisely what was needed for the role. All of these candidates had graduate degrees, one even a Ph.D. And all of them exceeded the minimum experience for the job. I was astonished when the CIO told me and the rest of the hiring committee, "these candidates were overqualified."

First of all, let me make something very clear here. There is no such thing as an overqualified candidate for any position. When questioned about this, the CIO stated he was "afraid that these candidates might not find the position meaningful enough to stay, since they were so educated." I noticed the candidates chosen by the CIO for interviews had less education and experience than he did. Mr. Rumsfeld's axiom was very accurate, in this example. Perhaps the new hire with the Ph.D. would not stay forever. Still, I bet they would have been great at their role in the organization while they were there, and the value they could add would be well worth the risk compared to the risk taken by the CIO in hiring the less qualified candidates. You really don't know. For all one knows, they may have wanted that role to be a role they stayed in long-term.

If you are doing your job correctly, those employees will remain with your organization a lot longer than you think they will. I have personally seen and had employees tell me that even though they know they can get more money somewhere else, they stay because of the great culture and environment working for my IT group. The hiring CIO I was consulting for just wanted a warm body in a position to take his orders and be his minion. He may have assumed going cheap and low bar would help the bottom line. I'm not sure what was going through his mind. However, It is extremely rare to bring on mediocre managers and successfully mentor them to be stellar without a lot off effort on your part. You and your organization will be far better of starting with the best and fine tuning.

Hire the best! Hire what I call complementary excellence. Those are managers who complement your IT group, your vision, your philosophy, and are the best of the best, independent thinking, and experienced [A] people who bring fresh ideas to the table—especially if they have strengths that balance your own weaknesses. You must have competent deputies, directors, managers, supervisors, and staff, who can be mentored to one day become a skilled supervisor and on up, maybe even replacing you someday. You cannot build a great culture if you don't follow that principle. If you hire the best and find you can't retain them, you may want to start fixing the issue by looking squarely in the mirror first. Bad leaders and bad managers cause high turn-over and low productivity.

Several studies[1] indicate that 65% of employees would rather have a new manager than a pay raise. Three out of four employees report their manager is the worst and most stressful part of their job. Great CIOs are leaders who can adapt to their staff's different leadership requirements and respond appropriately. The opposite is true of poor leaders, who will not trust anyone on their team and believe responsibility and accountability are delegated along with authority. Rather than using any mistake as a learning tool, leaders like Fred will make statements about "staff making them look bad." Or "making them look like the bad guy." This, of course, tends to demoralize staff even further. When I first took over as the CIO for the City of Chattanooga, one of my employees told me there was a significant difference between myself and my predecessor. When my predecessor made a mistake, he would yell and blame his staff for not doing something correctly or misinterpreting what he wanted—which I was told most of time was due to unrealistic expectations. On the contrary, I took responsibility for my mistake that day and the blame for the team's failure was on me; and, I made it a point to say so.

Hiring Isn't a Perfect Practice

So, what do you do if you make a hiring mistake? We've all been there. You sift through hundreds of applicants trying to narrow the field down, and you find the perfect candidate who looks good on paper, interviewed well, impressed your colleagues, and generally fits the bill. A year later, you are regretting your hiring decision. Don't worry, it happens. It's hard to tell a lot about a person in just a few hours of interviews. I've done that a few times, and could likely do it again. The reality of hiring for the public sector can shock some, especially if coming in from the private sector. It is challenging to find great people, given the hiring restrictions and procedures some public sector agencies follow. People dedicated to public service, willing to work for less pay, and are intelligent and reliable enough to do well, can be rare.

When you need to discipline or remove people, you may also need to jump through many fiery hoops. You may be wondering why it is so complicated to remove bad apples in the public sector. This reality is in part due to a landmark case back in 1985; Cleveland Board of Education v. Loudermill. Doesn't mean you can't fire people or discipline them; it just means you must provide them adequate notice of the action and the ability to respond (i.e. a loudermill hearing). You should always follow your organization's generally accepted human resource practices, and of course, federal employment laws. However, don't sit back and let bad managers continue to be bad managers. Train them and mentor them if you can and they are willing; everyone deserves a shot. If that doesn't work, get them out of there as quickly as possible because they are like poison to your staff. They may disrupt or destroy the very mission you are working towards.

ENVIRONMENT OF TRUST

Hiring new people in your IT group—at any level— is the same as coming on as a new CIO, which brings us full circle to an environment of trust. Earlier, I discussed the first impressions of your staff and how important building trust was. One crucial factor in building trust, and ultimately a great culture, is learning to let go and trust your experts. As the CIO, you do not, I repeat, DO NOT, need to know everything at all times or be the smartest person in the room. Great CIOs trust their staff to do the job and appropriately delegate the authority for them to do so. After all, you hired the best, right? So, back off and let them do their job. Telling people how to do their job is not the same thing as mentoring them to be great leaders. Don't confuse micromanagement with mentoring. CIOs with poor leadership skills want people to think they are the supreme expert and know every detail of their IT operation at all times with the ability to handle every situation, or at least maintain that illusion to their boss. These leadership poor CIOs are untrusting grandiloquent people who will gladly tell you how to do your job, then toss you under the bus to save their own skin when things go awry.

That is not to say CIOs can't be knowledgeable about their IT group's operations and may still have expertise in a specific subject. That's different. However, great CIOs are not worried about the day-to-day responsibilities of subordinate staff. Instead, they focus on the strategy, planning, budget, and performance of the IT portfolio driving value in the organization and help meet its strategic objectives. Great CIOs, or any leader for that matter, don't see their staff working for them. Great CIOs work for their staff. They worry about breaking down barriers to the team's success, working towards compromise, and building relationships with other organizational areas. As the CIO, you must chart the course. If you hired and trained the best staff you can find, let them worry about keeping the ship afloat and steaming ahead. You stay on the bridge, where the captain of the ship belongs. These concepts become more critical the larger your staff size gets, especially if your staff sizes from 100 to upwards of 500 or more IT staff. That's when it is critical to focus on leadership and your management teams.

You Work for the Staff

Great CIOs create a trusting environment, where the emphasis is not to look for blame, definitely not to blame people, but to seek out and fix broken processes or systems instead—to continually improve. These CIOs seek constant and honest feedback from their staff, at all levels and don't punish staff for being honest.

This is especially if it is constructive criticism about you. In an open and trusting environment, staff will thrive. It is also worth mentioning, you may learn a little bit more about yourself in the process. I know I did.

Along these same lines, the CIO must never punish bad information, a.k.a. "shooting the messenger." If you get angry and yell or blame and chastise people for bringing you bad news, then your staff will eventually stop bringing you bad news. You will be effectively cut off from the pulse of your team and any actual situation going on. Staff will actually go out of their way to avoid you unless they have some good news—maybe not even then if you're really terrible about it. If you are left in the dark, your decisions will be affected and cause more extensive problems down the road. A great CIO must create a welcoming and safe environment where management and staff can speak freely, even when the news isn't the greatest. This is true of failures as well, but more on that later.

Ironically, I have had people in the public sector tell me that this is a pipe dream. Not surprisingly, they are shocked when I tell them they are obviously not doing something correctly, are not fully trusting their staff, or have hired the wrong people, which goes right back to not doing something correctly. I suggested they may want to do a little self-reflection first.

Douglas McGregor's Theory X & Theory Y of motivation defines that CIO's way of thinking as an X mentality. This theory dictates people are inherently lazy and can't be trusted to do what they need to do. Thus, the leader/manager must step in and keep the lazy worker in check, at all times, to properly motivate the worker. It is one of the absolute worst traits to have in a leader, in my opinion. If you want better motivation for staff, don't be a Theory X boss.

This brings me to another critical factor in building a great culture: reducing, or if possible eliminating, communication silos and bureaucracy within the IT group. Wait, you say, eliminate bureaucracy in government? Yes! Do it as much as possible, especially when it comes to communication, at the very least. Poor CIOs will attempt to control every communication by enacting high levels of bureaucracy in the IT group. I've seen this too many times, and perhaps you have also. Every idea or concept must be vetted and approved by the CIO before it ever leaves the IT group. The CIO retains ultimate control over everything and wants none of their staff to speak with anyone outside of the department, especially anyone who is a peer or above them in "rank." To compound matters, in order to get information to the CIO from anywhere else in the IT group, you must first speak to a supervisor, who in turn talks to the manager, who then speaks to the director, who speaks to the deputy CIO, and then finally the CIO. All this tends to do is create colossal information gaps and large productivity bottlenecks. Creativity and critical thinking are severely crippled under a poor leader. If left unchecked, this behavior just feeds the totalitarian reactive state the IT group will inevitably become. Communication, straightforward communication, is critical. Anyone in my IT group can bring ideas to the table, bring up problems they have discovered, and provide solutions to these problems. No organization is ever perfect. Even when you fill in performance gaps and get to a great state, you will still need to eventually adapt and improve. Allowing your staff to openly communicate and think freely will make this process seem effortless in the long run.

BE AN OPEN COMMUNICATOR

Great CIOs are highly effective communicators and connect with people at all levels of the organization. They listen well and provide genuine and sincere feedback. On the contrary, poor CIOs do very little, if any, communicating. They tend to be more order-giving and are not effective listeners. Their feedback, when given, is forced and insincere. These CIOs tend to not tolerate much inquiry as to their methods either. Good communication is essential to success for any role in any organization, but especially for leaders. Good communication is more than typing up a few emails or picking up the phone now and again. To be a good communicator, you need to be adept at listening and actively participating in the conversation. You also need to get out of your office and talk to people throughout the organization. If you are remote working, get on a quick Zoom session—or whatever you prefer to use—and speak face-to-face. If you don't have your finger on the organization's pulse, you won't know what strategies to apply or tactics to implement to get your IT group adding value to the organization.

FAKE NOT THE COMMUNICATION YOU WILL

As a leader, you also need to be aware that you cannot fake good communication skills. Trust me when I tell you that pretending to listen will not work. The person you are communicating with will see right through your facade, no matter how good an actor you may think you are. It actually becomes even more evident to the person you are genuinely insincere. Your body language and posturing will give you away every time, and there is not much one can do to hide that. If you have ever had a funny feeling that this person was full of it, or they seemed oblivious to what was taking place, then you actually know what I am referring to. You just might not have realized why. You get a funny feeling because of subtle cues in a person's body language you pick up subconsciously. Or it could just be the fact they spent the entire conversation typing on their smartphone then asked you to repeat yourself. Either way, you notice.

IDEAS COME FROM ANYWHERE

Communication is more than just talking about what IT is doing and sending those messages down or up the command chain. Great CIOs also know, great ideas come from the most unlikely places and open communication doors up to anyone. I love hearing thoughts from front-line staff and anyone in-between, even if they don't work in IT. Some of the best innovative ideas in several of the organizations I have worked for have come from the most unlikely staff, some of whom were not in IT. I have a proper open-door policy and encourage staff from any level to see me whenever and for whatever reason. It is not uncommon for me to have someone come in and just toss out an idea, even in a one-sided conversation with themselves, only using me in a soundboard sort of way. People sometimes leave saying, "thanks for hearing me out. I think I figured out the problem," before I've even figured out what they are talking about.

People like to know you are open enough to just let them come by and bounce an idea off you or quickly gripe about a project problem. Problems are significant. If your staff doesn't want to come to you with problems, then something is wrong. And as I have previously stated, you will soon find yourself in trouble. General Colin Powell, former U.S. Secretary of State, former Chairman of the Joint Chiefs, former National Security Advisor, and retired U.S. Army Four-Star General, said, *"Leadership is solving problems. The day soldiers stop bringing you their problems is the day you have stopped leading them. They have either lost confidence that you can help or concluded you do not care. Either case is a failure of leadership."*

When your staff comes to you, be genuine and listen to them—hear them. When a member of my team does stop by, I always make sure I stop whatever I am doing, turn and look at them when they are talking. I am genuinely interested in what they have to say. You're the CIO and can get busy. Staff understand and will even be okay if you are unable to talk with them right away. However, if you are still typing an email and nodding your head while mumbling, "uh-huh," you will be sending the wrong message. There are plenty of times when I'm too busy to talk, need to finish getting my thoughts down , or finish reading something. That's okay, but tell them you will be with them in a moment, find a good stopping point, and give them your undivided attention. This should be a no-brainer. However, you might be surprised at how many CIOs and IT managers I have seen doing this. By taking a few minutes out of your day to truly hear someone's problems and help them, you send a compelling message as a strong leader. Demonstrate your openness and willingness to just be a decent human being who happens to be in charge, rather than the boss no one wants.

This chapter's concepts are just the beginning of building a great culture. In the following chapters, I will discuss everything else needed to create a great culture. Everything you do from here on out either goes towards building a great culture and adding value or going in the opposite direction.

CHAPTER THREE
IT'S ALL ABOUT THE PEOPLE

"*I get by with a little help from my friends***" - John Lennon & Paul McCartney**

There is a lot we can automate throughout an organization. However, we still need people. You can't really do this by yourself—well, I know some small rural agencies out there may only have two to maybe ten IT staff, so you kind of have to do it on your own in those cases. For the larger agencies, where more of the problems with these topics are, you really can't do this yourself. I've already discussed the need to hire [A] people. Yet, you still have to go further than just hiring great people for a great culture; you need to support them too. Remember, part of your role as the CIO is to work for your staff, which can sometimes be challenging. This chapter will show you a few things that can help with staff motivation and esprit de corps, driving innovation.

PROMOTIONAL PATHS

One of the things you should do is look at what promotional opportunities your staff have. Some people get to a certain point in their professional career and they are comfortable right where they are. And that is fine so long as they are continuing to be productive and fully participative in the IT group. Most people are ambitious and strive for more significant challenges and achievements. Unfortunately, the public sector isn't always geared for this, especially at the local government level. You will frequently find no promotional opportunities unless someone in a higher position retires, leaves or moves up themselves. This can be detrimental to the IT group's morale and subsequently affect performance throughout the IT group.

Some agencies have worked on this problem by creating career paths for all staff. All positions across these organizations are handled much like the federal government—similar to some police and fire departments, as well. The thing to remember in any such case is you clearly define the path a person can take from an entry-level position, right out of school to becoming the CIO. Every step that must be taken, the amount of time-in-grade, the level of education needed to move up, certifications, demonstrated knowledge, and so on. As much as we love our HR folks, this is not something they can or should define. It should be the CIO and their experts, in-house and in the industry to describe all this. I know of some public sector agencies that will

38

allow reclassifying positions while people are in them; but, that is usually rare in my experience. So in those situations, it can be beneficial to leave at least one—for smaller IT groups—or more positions vacant. Doing so will preserve the ability to reclassify a vacancy to a higher or different classification, where there may be an opportunity for one or more internal candidates to move up. You can get creative with this approach and allow for advancement. However, always follow all organizational policies, procedures, and hiring laws.

Define your promotional paths to be as straightforward as possible. A great example is how the military handles promotions and availability. All branches of the military traditionally had an "up or out" mentality. It was unfortunate, because I knew many Captains who were very good at their job, but if they didn't make Major, they were discharged from the service. I am really referring to how military pay grades are structured more so than highlighting the up or out mentality. Every branch uses the same type of pay grade; Enlisted grades are E-1 through E-9. Warrant Officer grades are WO-1 through WO-5—except the Navy and Air Force. And Commissioned Officers are O-1 through O-10 in all military branches. Do not confuse rank with pay grades. They are not the same thing because some pay grades can have more than one rank. For example, an Army E-4 can be a Specialist or a Corporal depending on the duties, assignment, and needs of the unit. It is the same for other pay grades across all branches. However, I won't get into those details, as it isn't relevant to the topic. What is good about the pay grades is each one has a specified list of requirements to move to the next pay grade.

In most military branches, the first few grades increases, both enlisted and officer, are automatically achieved based on time in grade, with a few exceptions. Anything past that point has to be qualified for. For example, moving from E-1 to E-4 in the Army is automatic. They are not considered supervisory positions—exception is E-4 corporal and infrequent. O-1 to O-3 are also automatic based on time-in-grade. That's what I meant earlier when I said if you don't make—qualify for and beat the competition—O-4 Major, then you're out. As you go higher and higher up the chain of command, there are fewer available slots. The same can be said for local government. There is usually only one chief. However, there could be several deputy chiefs, assistant chiefs, directors, managers, supervisors, etc.

For the IT group, you want to have various levels for your staff to work through. Let's start with your applications group as our first example. You could have an entry-level position we will call a Software Development Engineer 1 (SDE1). This position does not have any certification requirements, requires only a basic college education (e.g. associates degree and an entry-level skill set). You should find candidates for these positions relatively easily in most areas if your pay scale is close to the market average. Your next level on the applications ladder would be an SDE2, then SDE3, and finally a SDE4. I don't recommend going above a level 4 or 5 before you get into supervisory positions because it's just too many levels in my professional opinion. I stopped at level 4 in my IT group. Each step up the ladder requires more education, more time-in-grade, perhaps certification, and other such requirements. By doing this, you are doing two things. First, you clearly define what is needed to move up the ladder, so there is no ambiguity between positions. I have seen two different sets of level one and level two classes that read the exact same with only one difference between them, knowing a specific system. So, be sure to clearly differentiate the difference between a whatever position one through four. Second, it helps build your staff knowledge up by encouraging them to strive for more and take on new and exciting challenges. After all, one of your goals as CIO is to develop several possible replacements for you internally. So start at the bottom and encourage the next generation of leaders to step up.

You can do this for all areas of the IT group. With your software folks and the aforementioned SDE levels, you could have Scrum Master 1 through 4. You could have Applications Specialist 1 through 4 or Systems Analyst 1 through 4. On the networking and infrastructure side, you could establish Network Engineer 1 through 4, and perhaps Systems Specialist 1 through 4 for your systems folks who maintain your servers, patching, etc. This also applies to security staff, with Security Analyst 1 through 4. All of these specialty lines should then go on up to supervisory positions (e.g. Applications Supervisor, Network Supervisor), middle management positions (e.g. Applications Manager, IT Security

Manager, etc.), director positions (e.g Director of IT Operations, etc.), then Deputy CIO positions all the way to CIO. There are many positions in the IT group, so I won't touch on all of them, but you get the idea. It is up to you to decide what works best for your IT group with positions and advancement requirements. Just make sure they are fair, achievable, and consistent. Also, it is essential to note that simply because someone is qualified to take on the next role doesn't always mean they should. This is what is known as the Peter principle, where someone is a rock star at X position. As a result, you move them to a higher, usually supervisory role, and suddenly they seem like they are barely able to keep their head above the water, hating their job as a result.

Fair Pay

Pay is also another sore spot for a lot of CIOs across the nation. Unfortunately, some public sector agencies have not kept their pay scales up to par with the private sector. It is difficult enough to find and retain great people working in technology to recruit to the public sector, much less convincing them to work for far less than their counterparts in the private sector. As a CIO, you may know this and relay this to your leaders; and, there very well may be nothing that can or will be done to change it, depending on the leadership. Perhaps, if you are in one of those situations, suggest a compensation study to your head of HR. In unison, let's give a great big thank you to those agencies who have kept up.

You have done the first thing in finding and hiring the very best for your organization realizing compensation is competitive and the public sector must be competitive to keep up.

THE ENVIRONMENT

Part of working for your staff is creating a working environment they enjoy coming to and working in. This should not be confused with building a great culture. Having an open and welcoming work environment is part of making that culture. The best way I can explain this is to describe the work environment at the City of Chattanooga's IT department. Chattanooga's IT workspace is an open floor design, with open desks and workstations, not closed-off cubicles, conference rooms off to the side, and a large conference table in the middle of the floor between desks and gathering areas. At the time of this writing, we had the entire 3rd floor of the Edney Innovation Center, only one block from city hall, as headquarters and smaller spaces in several other buildings. The desks are spaced according to the area. And, specific teams clump together on the open floor.

I held our Monday leadership meeting in the center of the building's floor, at a conference area we dubbed *Area 51*. This meeting is required for supervisory staff and up. Since it is held in the middle of the entire floor, anyone sitting nearby can listen in. The topics discussed are planning issues regarding projects, budget, deployments, innovation ideas, leadership practices, etc. These are all topics anyone in the department can participate in at any time. During the COVID-19 pandemic, even the Zoom invite on the calendar was open for all IT, as well as, other employees of the city. To keep things on track, we used an agenda that anyone in the department can add items of significance to, which we get to after hitting the regular agenda items.

As for meetings, we tend to hold the "less is more" philosophy scheduling regular meetings only when needed. We also have a no meetings on Friday's rule. Unless it is vital, no meetings should be scheduled on Fridays. This isn't always possible, but what this rule does is twofold. First, it leaves everyone's Fridays open for those times where getting together is critical. Second, it gives everyone in the IT group the chance to finish up the remainder of their week's work, which would otherwise linger until Monday; or some may take work home with them. It's good for staff morale to have the weekends for their families or themselves and not think about work, and it feels good to end the week without the stress of watching the clock and calendar all day. Of course the nature of our work means there are a few exceptions to this rule.

We have several other policies in place that are designed to improve staff morale and create a relaxed environment in which to work. While people can choose to have a specific desk and workspace, the open and comfortable floor plans with comfortable seating arrangements allows staff to find a cozy corner, put on headphones, and work the way they want to work. No one questions where people are or why they are not at their desk. Staff can also work from practically wherever they want. It is not uncommon for me to walk around the downtown area, to and from meetings or to the local sandwich or coffee shop, and see several of my staff huddled in a corner, heads down, typing away or conversing over a latte about an upcoming software launch. I see them practically everywhere, and guess what? I say hi and don't question what they are doing, nor does anyone else in the IT group or the rest of the city, for that matter. The IT staff at Chattanooga are very productive. In fact, our productivity jumped nearly 27% after I first instituted the work from anywhere policy. Think about it this way; we are all adults; and no one likes having someone question what they are doing all the time or looking over their shoulder all day. You know what you are supposed to do, and you, in theory, will do it. The CIOs and managers who think an employee must be seated at their desk eight hours a day and account for all their time need to take a step back and realize it does not work that way. Instead, it actually kills productivity. I've noticed, trying to force people to put in a full eight-hour day heads down at their desk actually reduces overall output, something tech companies in the private sector have known since the early 2000's.

Inspiration comes from many places. Letting people be human and treating them like adults not only makes them feel appreciated, but make them want to work and be part of the big picture. If it makes you feel better, look at it from a financial perspective. The truth is when a firm hires employees, they don't hire them to sit at a desk for eight hours a day, pretending to be productive. They hire them to actually be productive. The keyword there is produce. If an expected outcome is completed on time and under budget, plus other ideas that can help the organization come out of the deal for the same investment, why do you care if an employee is sitting in a coffee shop or in the corner with headphones on instead of at their desk all day? Why would you care if they stared out the window for 20 minutes after lunch or played a video game, had a conversation in a hallway or any number of other things some managers seem to constantly be worried about. People work harder and faster when you just let them work how they want to work and treat them like adults. All you have to do is hold them accountable and expect results.

95% of employees will produce more than you thought possible. And, yes, there will always be those who will take advantage of the policy because there will always be lazy people or those who work harder at getting out of work than just doing what needs to be done. If you have folks like that, again, weed them out and get rid of them. You will always know who is pulling their weight and working, especially in agile environments. However, this technique does not always work well for all positions. It is sometimes challenging to balance the service desk staff responsibilities because of the nature of the work—being on-call all day and sometimes all night. However, having enough staff to balance the workload helps, and it also helps if occasionally the techs get to spend a week in ops, or with the developers, or even shadowing you. Following and getting a feel for other IT group areas works well to help staff decide a career path, while also helping to build skill sets and trust. After all, they are IT's future, as in most cases with entry-level positions. And some staff, if not most, will go on to move into security, or networking, or software engineering, etc.

Ms. Pac-Man

My favorite part of Chattanooga's IT work environment—which I must say I too occasionally took advantage of between meetings—is the custom, in-house-built, arcade console. It is an entire upright, old school Ms. Pac-Man cabinet, complete with the original boards and memory chips one of my directors found in a storage room at the main library branch. The library was going to throw it out; so, we procured it. One of our very talented staff built a fully working machine out of it, using a flat-screen monitor and a raspberry pie. Another employee made a custom etched dash for the controls. Now, the staff has a home-made, fully functioning '80s retro game machine that will play any of the hundreds of old arcade games some of us older geeks played as kids. We even have challenges on some games for the high score, like Ms. Pac-Man, since that's what the side of the cabinet says. People come and go at the machine; and, it isn't unusual to see a few folks gather around it having fun. Of course, this was all before the COVID-19 pandemic of 2020. I'm curious to see how things will work going forward since our work environment has shifted to us all being at home 99% of the time and will likely stay that way.

SLEEPING ON THE JOB

We had one policy I called the siesta rule, which stated anyone in IT may take a 30-minute power nap at a location of their choice, between 11:00 AM and 2:00 PM. We had people napping in the conference room and on one of the couches during lunch for a while. This got to be somewhat controversial, with certain other departments complaining that some IT staff were sleeping on the job. Even when it was explained departmental policy allowed this to happen, it still didn't go over well. We were not told to stop doing it, officially. However, it did start to hamper some of our relationships with other departments. Technically, City policy was no sleeping on the job... so that too raised a few eyebrows since it skirted the line between city policy and my ability to set departmental policy. Regardless, use it as an example of creative ways to think outside of the norm, break the status quo, and create an excellent environment for your staff. We, as leaders, try to make these highly functional work environments. Unfortunately, the public sector still has some hurdles to overcome. Primarily because of politics and what it looks like when a government employee is "sleeping on the job." It can give the wrong impression, especially for those looking for excuses to complain about the government or find someone abusing something. They are out there in droves, and for good reason. You can thank all the idiots who came before us and abused their role for personal gain.

ALTERNATIVE METHODS OF REWARDS

I've said before, catch people doing things right, not doing something wrong, and reward them appropriately. Everyone likes a good pat on the back occasionally to know they are moving in the right direction. You typically can't give raises on-the-fly in the public sector. However, you can provide praises in unique ways. One unfortunate thing for most government agencies is the inability to raise someone's salary or give bonuses based on merit. Again, because of all the idiots who came before us and abused the system giving friends raises and other things they shouldn't have been given. Everyone in all agencies across the board should get cost of living allocations (COLA) every year to keep up with inflation if the budget allows for it. In addition, I also highly suggest some form of merit-based increases.

Some agencies, including one I used to work for, do performance evaluations every six months. The annual evaluation result potentially adds to the base cost of living allocation with a merit raise. There is a three level rating, ranging from needs improvement, meets expectations, or exceeds expectations. If an employee gets a needs improvement on their annual evaluation, they only receive the base cost of living allocation. If an employee receives a meets expectations rating—a good thing—they get the cost of living allocation and a 3% merit raise. And an exceeds expectations evaluation warrants an additional 3% above the cost of living allocation and meets expectations merit raise, totaling 6% above the COLA. I've seen several variations on this model, including one where you got nothing at all, not even a cost of living allowance, if you got a needs improvement rating. Meets expectations got you. the cost of living allocation and exceeds expectations got you some percentage above the cost of living allocation—usually 3%.

Despite my preference for this merit raise model, I am actually not a fan of written evaluations. Primarily when they are not performed correctly or worse performed by a micro-manager who waits till the evaluation six to twelve months later to tell you didn't perform your job correctly. Written evaluations add undue stress to an employee, especially when they don't get realistic or constant feedback and direct communication from their immediate supervisor. While they tend to serve a documentation purpose in the public sector—refer to Loudermill hearings—I still don't like them. I prefer the method of instant feedback. If something is wrong, say so right then and there. I'm not talking about chastising or belittling an employee in front of people either. If they are doing something right and doing it well, praise them and reward them—that you can do in front of the rest of the staff. If they are under-performing, take them aside right when you notice, ask them what's going on, get their input on why their performance is lacking in whatever area. There may be a personal or other reason you might not be aware of—yes, people's private lives bleed into work just as much as work can affect home life. If not, get to the bottom of it right then, don't wait six months or a year for the formal evaluation to say something. That just exacerbates the stress of the written evaluation. Either way, with or without written evaluations, it would be nice if you could have some control over merit increases as the CIO.

Some argue merit raises are not really fair to all. I say bull shit! If you treat the low-performance employees the same as the highly productive employees, you diminish the high-performing employee's performance, reducing morale and setting the wrong precedent for employees long-term. Remember, our job is not to make all employees happy. Our job is to ensure the IT group is productive and providing value to the organization. While you want fairness in policy and procedures, you also want fairness to your employee's work ethics and productivity. Award those who produce and help and mentor those who don't to become producers. If they still can't become producers, it's not fair to reward them the same as the high producing employees. This is really management 101 stuff, and notice I didn't say leadership? That's because these aren't leadership techniques or traits; they are management functions and equally as important.

So, maybe you can, or perhaps you can't, offer merit-based raises each year. Regardless, there are still other ways you can reward employees for excellence. The IT group for the City of Chattanooga has an awards program that has several different levels. At the beginning of the year, we have an awards ceremony where the top folks nominated and chosen for outstanding work get awarded either a pin or a challenge coin—top award. The following is the exact excerpt from the Chattanooga IT group's awards section in their operations manual.

///

Why Awards Are Made.

DIT awards are designed to recognize excellence, service, and program achievements. Prompt recognition through the presentation of awards earned will promote esprit de corps within the department.

Eligibility:

A DIT staff member must be in good standing at the time of the distinguished act and must meet the criteria established for the award. All award recommendations must be submitted within 1 year of the act's termination date, achievement, or service performed.

Repetitive Awards:

Only one award will be made for a single meritorious achievement or one continuous period of meritorious service. Subsequent awards of the same type are permitted for subsequent acts.

Who May Initiate Recommendations:

Any City employee having knowledge of an act or service meriting recognition may initiate a recommendation for an award.

How to Initiate Recommendations:

Recommendations will be submitted through the nomination form. Care should be exercised to ensure all items are complete. The justification for the award will be included as a narrative statement and should be specific as to inclusive dates, places, and facts relating to the act, achievement, or service. The narrative must clearly portray how the individual's achievements meet or exceed the criteria set forth for the selected award. The award review board may recommend a higher or lower award based on the eligibility and specific act.

Award Presentations

All awards will be presented during a regular or special DIT staff meeting or special awards ceremony. MoWa is a separate award and can only be presented at the February DIT staff meeting in the year following the award. e.g., the 2018 MoWa Award was given for the year 2018 in February 2019.

CIO's Award for Excellence (CAFE.)

The highest achievement any member of DIT can achieve. For outstanding achievement or meritorious service rendered specifically on behalf of the City of Chattanooga or its citizens. In itself, the superior performance of routine duties does not constitute automatic justification for the CIO Award for Excellence. Awards should be restricted to recognizing achievements and services that are clearly outstanding and unmistakably exceptional compared to similar achievements and accomplishments of personnel of like rank and responsibilities. In instances where many individuals are affiliated with an exceptionally successful program, project, or operation, the CIO Award for Excellence should be awarded to the relatively few individuals whose contributions clearly stand out from the others and who have contributed most to the success of the program, project or operation. The CIO Award for Excellence differs from the DIT Commendation Award in that it recognizes excellent achievements and service significantly above and beyond typical duty performance.

The award consists of two paid personal days, an individually numbered gold challenge coin, matching gold lapel pin, and numbered certificate. Recipients of this award are authorized to wear the Gold DIT lanyard in place of the standard Grey or MoWa Orange to designate the award's achievement. It may only be awarded by the CIO or higher authority.

DIT Motivated Warrior Award (MoWa)

Warrior: noun

1. ~~a person engaged or experienced in warfare; soldier.~~
2. *a person who shows or has shown great vigor, courage, or aggressiveness, as in politics or athletics.*

DIT Warriors are the most motivated individuals on any program, project, or operation in the Dept. of Information Technology within a specific year. MoWa recipients will follow and champion the DIT mission, uphold the department motto, uphold the department core values, provide productive feedback at all levels of the organization, and may be a recipient of multiple DIT awards in the given year. The MoWa Award is the DIT equivalent to an "Employee of the Year" award.

The MoWa award comes with dedicated gated parking space for one year, plus one paid personal day.

DIT Commendation Award (DITCom)

Outstanding duty performance where achievements and services are clearly and unmistakably exceptional compared to similar achievements and service of staff of like position, rank, and responsibility. In instances where several members are affiliated with an exceptionally successful program, project or operation, the DIT Commendation Award will be awarded only to those who clearly stand out from the others and who contributed most to the program's success or operation. It may be presented by the DCIO or CIO.

The DITCom comes with a silver lapel pin. One paid personal day or the option to break the personal day into increments of four hours.

DIT Achievement Award (DITAch)

Presented for outstanding duty performance or service to the Department of Information Technology by a member of DIT.

The DITAch comes with a bronze lapel pin and four hours of paid personal time.

DIT Customer Service Agent of the Year

Presented to any member of DIT in recognition for the most accumulation of customer service awards within a year, the highest service rating for the year, and highest met levels of SLAs for the year. The recipient of the Customer Service Agent of the Year also gets to park in the CIO's parking spot for two weeks and the Deputy CIO's parking space for an additional two weeks.

DIT Customer Service Award (CSA)

Presented to any member of DIT in recognition for excellent customer service and comes with two paid hours of personal time.

The criteria are as follows.

1. Exceed 98% of the Service Level Agreement standards for the month;
2. Expeditious resolution of service requests or incidents;
3. Expeditious, consistent, and thorough communication with users and staff on each service request;
4. Satisfactory ITOPS customer survey results of 4.0 stars or greater average for the month;
5. Positive written and verbal user feedback throughout the month (email, conversation, or submitted complete survey).

Certificate of Appreciation

Presented to any member of DIT or other City Employee by DIT for the recognition of a specific duty or responsibility during a project, program, or large operation.

The criteria for each award and the resulting prize to go with it are clearly defined. Thus everyone in the IT group knows precisely how to achieve those awards. It may be a simple thing, but giving up your parking space for two weeks each year to one of the lowest-paid employees in the IT group speaks volumes and is a real morale booster. Post-COVID, since most of my staff will remain remote working for the most part, we will have to come up with alternative prizes.

\\\

One last way to build morale I will mention is after our staff meetings. Our monthly staff meetings are to disseminate information and bring the various divisions of the IT group, who may not work with each other regularly, together. We also use this time for team-building exercises or quick fun games. This was especially important during 2020-2021, where COVID-19 had everyone tucked in at home and social distancing. Even just getting on a Zoom call with all the staff at the same time has an impact on morale. We did background themes for those Zoom meetings, such as displaying a background representing your favorite 80's movie, favorite video game, favorite instrument, pet, adult beverage, candy, and so forth. We would have conversations about these items for a bit during the beginning of meetings as people were joining. After all the information was disseminated and if a game was competitive, I usually let the winners of the challenge go home, or in the case of remote working from home, just stop working an hour early. Everyone else could leave 45 mins early or something to that effect. Each of these methods works towards building a great culture and working environment, keeping staff motivated, productive and innovative.

PART TWO

STRATEGIZE AND MEASURE

CHAPTER FOUR
THE ASSESSMENT

"Stay diagnostic even as you take action." ~ Ronald Heifetz

I started this book off with leadership and the importance of building a great culture, because those topics are core to doing anything else I will discuss in later chapters. And even though you start to develop—or deteriorate—a great environment the minute you walk through the door as the IT group's new CIO, you still need a full assessment of the organization and the IT group to be successful. Keep those leadership lessons in mind when you start your review.

So, what is an assessment? An assessment is a formal process by which you determine the organization's current state and your IT group's condition, based on your observations against the IT core competencies. This is an absolutely crucial step in the entire strategic planning process. If you don't know where you stand, you have no idea where to go from there. The assessment process is straightforward, and you may already be doing something similar without formally writing it down. It is an iterative process;

so, you can technically start anywhere. What exactly are you looking for? What are you really assessing? IT groups have 36 core competencies in four high-level groups and eight specific areas:

Strategy (HIGH-LEVEL GROUP)

    <u>Strategy & Governance</u> (SPECIFIC GROUPS)

        Management & Governance (COMPETENCIES)

        IT Strategy

        Enterprise Architecture

        Compliance & Controls

    <u>Value & Performance</u>

        Value Management

        Stakeholder Management

        Cost & Budgeting

        Vendor Management

Support

    <u>IT Organization & Policy</u>

        Organization Design

        Performance Management

        People Management

        Principles & Policy

Core (THE MEAT & POTATOES OF WHAT IT DOES)

    <u>Project & Service</u>

        Portfolio Management

        Project Management

        Service Management

        Quality & Continuous Improvement

Application Development
Requirements Gathering

Application Development

Application Maintenance

User Experience

Change Management

Release Management

Infrastructure & Operation
Manage Operations

Asset Management

Availability & Capacity

Service Desk

Problem Management

Cloud Strategy

Security & Risk
Risk Management

Security

Business Continuity & Disaster Recovery Planning

Data Architecture & Integrity

Enabler

Innovation & Analytics
Innovation Mandate

Business Innovation

Technology Innovation

Analytics & Reporting

To be thorough, you should do an evaluation on each of the 36 core competencies. Some are easy to assess, such as Business Continuity & DRP. That's as easy as putting hands on your IT group's continuing operations plan (COOP) and seeing when it was last updated, or if you even have one at all. Other competencies are a little more involved for a good assessment, such as Management & Governance. I'll walk through each one so you can see what you should be looking for.

Again this is an iterative process, so you don't have to start with the strategy group, but I usually do. Having these assessments in mind when working through the rest of the competencies, you begin to formulate your gap analysis in the back of your mind—more on gap analysis in a bit, The strategy group takes some time and probably will be an ongoing assessment, especially if you have a large staff and many operations. Go through each competency, ask questions, and be sure to take notes as you go along.

Strategy & Governance
1. Is there a formal governance process in place in the organization?
2. If so, what is the process?
3. Does the process make sense?
4. Does the process add value or slow things down?
5. Is the process documented?

IT Strategy
1. Does the organization have a formal strategic planning

process?

2. Does IT have a strategic planning process?
3. Does IT have an up-to-date strategic plan?
4. Is the process documented?
5. Are there IT mission and vision statements?
6. Are the mission and vision statements memorable, effective, and structured correctly?

Enterprise Architecture

7. Is IT using the enterprise architecture model or just "winging" it?
1. Is there a regular feedback loop in place?
2. Are enterprise discretionary or non-discretionary standards and policies in place, and are they used to determine business unit architecture?
3. Are any external discretionary or non-discretionary standards and guidelines used?

Compliance & Controls

4. Are all relevant policies or laws followed?
5. Does IT have a standards manual?
1. Does the organization have a standards manual?
2. Are internal or external audits performed regularly?
3. Are there any security controls in place?
4. Are all security controls followed?

Value Measurement

1. Is IT value measured?

2. Is IT value communicated?
3. Is it applied to stakeholders?

Stakeholder Management

1. Are stakeholders managed effectively?
2. Are stakeholders regularly communicated with?
3. Are stakeholders "on board"?

Cost & Budgeting

1. Is the budget kept sound?
2. Are the right things budgeted for?
3. Were there overages the previous budget year?
4. Is the budget audited?
5. Are costs managed well?
6. Are we paying for anything we no longer use or need?

Vendor Management

1. Are vendors audited?
2. Are contracts managed well?
3. Do we actively look for savings with vendors before renewing contracts?
4. Are we using the best vendors?

Organization Design

1. Is the IT group organizational structure effective?
2. Is it too complex?
3. Is the IT group Agile?

Performance Management

1. Is performance tracked?
2. Are key performance indicators (KPIs) meaningful and valuable?
3. Are metrics used to make changes that positively affect performance?
4. Are KPIs reported outside of the IT group?
5. Is performance discussed with IT, group staff?
6. Is there a performance dashboard?

People management

1. Are staff happy?
2. Are staff motivated?
3. Are staff productive?
4. Are supervisors and managers effective leaders?
5. Are staff suggestions taken?
6. Are staff given the freedom to speak freely?
7. Is there a clear career path for the team?

Principles & Policy

1. Does the IT group have a core set of principles?
2. Do staff know and follow the regulations?
3. Is there a policy manual?
4. Do staff read and sign off on the policies?
5. Are policies regularly reviewed and updated?
6. Do the policies make sense and are helpful?
7. Are the policies followed?

Portfolio Management

1. Is the IT group portfolio actively managed?
2. Is the IT portfolio actively measured for performance?
3. Are outcomes measured?
4. Do the projects make sense and are helpful?
5. Is the IT group included in the organization's portfolio management?

Service Management

1. Is the IT group service focused?
2. Does the IT group follow ITSM best practices? ITIL?
3. Is service looked at as a value add?
4. Are there service level agreements (SLAs) with partners?
5. Are the SLAs evaluated regularly?
6. Are there operations level agreements (OLAs) in place with vendors?
7. Do we use automated self-service technologies?

Quality & Continual Improvement

1. Does the IT group have quality management standards in place?
2. Are quality controls in place?
3. Do we look at our processes and procedures regularly?
4. Are staff permitted to change processes to be more efficient?

Requirements Gathering

1. Does the IT group use agile methods?
2. Do we have dedicated product owners?

3. Do we include stakeholders in the agile processes?
4. Do we follow best practices with gathering requirements?
5. Do we write use cases?
6. Are requirements checked against business processes?
7. Are business processes looked at before requirements are gathered?
8. Do we make business process re-engineering suggestions to stakeholders?
9. Do we follow systems engineering best practices?

Application Development
1. Do we use agile (Scrum)?
2. Do we have dedicated scrum masters?
3. Do we follow the software engineering body of knowledge (SWEBOK)?
4. Do we use pair programming techniques?
5. Do we use centralized source control?
6. Do we use centralized bug and code tracking (Jira)?
7. Do we measure development productivity (burn down charts, etc.)?
8. Do we code with security in mind?
9. Do we follow DevOps methods?

Application Maintenance
1. Do we track bugs and code changes?
2. Do we allow bugs to be reported from our apps?
3. Do we monitor code for security and compatibility issues?

4. Do we automate deployments (blue/green, etc.)
5. Are we virtualized?

User Experience

1. Do we have a dedicated UX designer?
2. Do we focus on UX rather than design?

Change Management

1. Do we have a formal change management process?
2. Is the process documented and understood by staff?
3. Is there a change approval process?
4. Are all changes verified and monitored?

Release Management

1. Do we use a blue/green deployment model (or similar)?
2. Do releases go through change management?
3. Are releases monitored and tracked?
4. Are releases pushed open a regular schedule?

Manage Operations

1. Do we have a clear plan for our infrastructure?
2. Are we virtualized and in the cloud?
3. Do we have a procedure manual?
4. Do staff follow the procedures?
5. Are operations efficient?

Asset Management

1. Do we have an accurate inventory?
2. Is the inventory up to date and monitored?

3. Is all equipment marked, tagged, or otherwise identified as belonging to the organization?
4. Is all equipment (that is not network equipment) assigned to a single person?
5. Is equipment accounted for when there is turnover?
6. Do we replace non-network equipment on a 3-year cycle?
7. Do we replace network equipment on a 5-year cycle?

Availability & Capacity
1. Do we monitor and measure network uptime?
2. Do we have an adequate bandwidth for all services and systems?
3. Are we staffed appropriately to handle a variety of situations? Emergencies?
4. Do we have redundancy built into the network? No single point of failure?

Service Desk
1. Do we measure customer service ratings?
2. Do we check KPIs and measure performance?
3. Do we have SLAs in place?
4. Do we monitor and adjust SLAs regularly?

Problem Management
1. Do we have a robust ticketing system?
2. Do we differentiate between incidents and issues?
3. Do we track all incidents and issues?
4. Do we provide consistent feedback to users?

5. Are we honest and forthcoming about issues and incidents reporting on them?

Cloud Strategy

1. Are we cloud-first?
2. Do we utilize cloud infrastructure (IaaS)?
3. Are we cloud-centric?

Risk Management

1. Do we have controls in place to monitor for risk?
2. Do we teach users about risks?
3. Do we test our infrastructure and other applications for risk?

Security

1. Is security first a mindset of the organization?
2. Business Continuity & DRP
3. Do we have a continuation of operations/disaster recovery plan (CooP/DR)?
4. Is the DR plan up to date?

Data Architecture & Integrity

1. What data is being stored?
2. Do we have a retention policy?
3. How is the data being stored?
4. Is personal protected information (PPI) retained?
5. Is PPI secured?
6. Are we capturing what we really need?

Innovation Mandate

1. Do we have a policy or mandate to innovate?
2. Do we encourage staff to look for and consistently improve/ enable change?
3. Are we change agents and fight the status quo?

Business Innovation

1. Do we look to improve business processes?
2. Do we look for ways to make conducting business with citizens better, faster, more efficient?
3. Do we encourage business units to improve?
4. Are we a catalyst for change?

Technology Innovation

1. Do we look to try and experiment with new or untested technologies?
2. Do we use ML/AI?
3. Are we a trendsetter in our field?

Analytics & Reporting

1. Do we have a data warehouse?
2. Do we mine data?
3. Do we look for trends and correlations with our data?
4. Do we have a metrics/KPI dashboard?
5. Do we assist other departments with analytics?
6. Does the organization have a performance management officer or team?

   Of course, you could ask several other questions for each

section; but, these are the essentials and a great starting point for assessing your IT group's core competencies. For customer service, if there is not already a performance management tracking mechanism in place that will give you a good idea of where your satisfaction ratings are, get one. You could always send out a quick survey to judge this and get a baseline to start. I provide some sample survey questions on the companion website (http://valuedrivenbook.com) you can use these samples as is, or modify them to meet your needs.

GAP ANALYSIS

After you have a complete assessment of your IT group, you should do some gap analysis on your worst competencies first. A gap analysis is a simple way for you to look at your current state. In this case, let's say service levels are lower than you would like—and the future state you want that competency to be at. For example, say your service satisfaction ratings are at 75%—don't laugh, I've seen worse—and you want them to be at least 95%. The gap in-between is where you strategize. You are trying to fill the performance gap; and the strategy is how you plan to do that.

///

GAP ANALYSIS TEMPLATE

Figure 4-1 shows a template you can use, which is also available for free on the companion website:

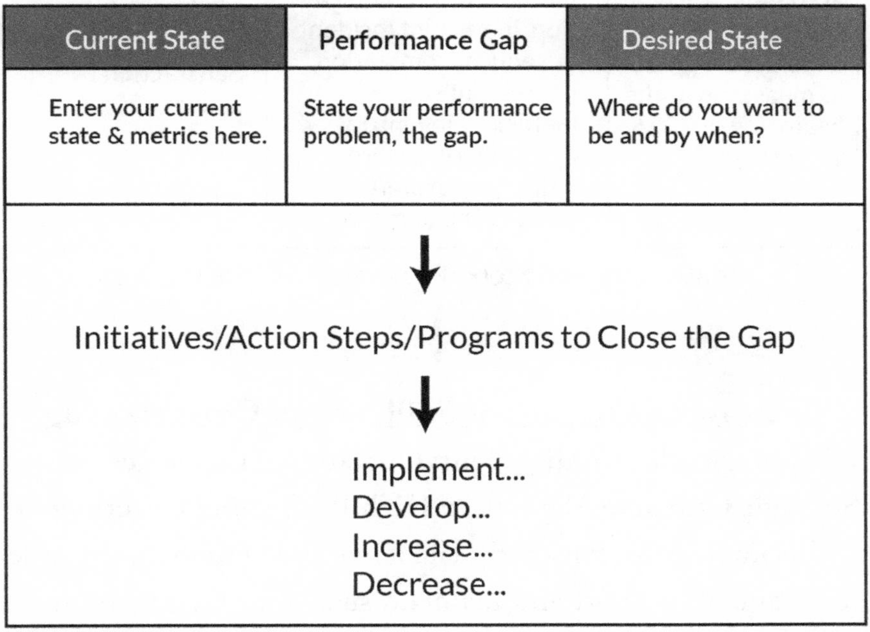

Current State	Performance Gap	Desired State
Enter your current state & metrics here.	State your performance problem, the gap.	Where do you want to be and by when?

↓

Initiatives/Action Steps/Programs to Close the Gap

↓

Implement...
Develop...
Increase...
Decrease...

Figure 4-1: Gap Analysis Template

Here is an example of a gap analysis we did in Chattanooga back when planning for the upcoming the FY 2016 budget year.

Current State	Performance Gap	Desired State
70.03% Customer Service Satisfaction (2015 - as measured at the beginning of 2016 via survey)	Inefficient communication, inefficient incident or request completion, limited skillset, inefficient inventory deployment, severe deficiency of staff to meet the demand.	**85%** or higher Customer Service Satisfaction by January 2017

Initiatives/Action Steps/Programs to Close the Gap

<u>Increase IT Operations Skill set and Cross training</u>

IT Strategic Theme Alignment: Operational Excellence

Strategic Outcome Alignment: High Performing Government

Technology is constantly changing and improving in order to be able to support and maintain such a progressive technical environment. IT personnel must have a formalized training process to promote expansion of capability and ensure cross training among personnel. Cross trained personnel will close the limited skill set gap. Enhancing the skills of our team will increase our customer service satisfaction by decreasing the mean time to recovery and increasing request and incident throughput.

Enhance Incident and Request Communication and Reporting Visibility

IT Strategic Theme Alignment: Operational Excellence

Strategic Outcome Alignment: High Performing Government

Transparency is important to measure performance against our customer service increase goals and communication is essential to increase performance. A new system has been put in place along with new processes that will enhance incoming support initiatives such as the Service Desk outsourcing.

Outsource IT Service Desk and Various Networking Positions

IT Strategic Theme Alignment: Operational Excellence

Strategic Outcome Alignment: High Performing Government

The main weakness in DIT's support structure is the lack of capability regarding the DIT's primary face to the City, the Service Desk. These staff lack the required skill sets, knowledge, and experience to adequately perform the needed duties. The networking staff are also in a similar position where skills are lacking enough to prevent common problems from being resolved quickly or the simple mitigation of complex issues that seem to arise in the form of frequent downtime. The strategy this year is to outsource specific commodity positions that can easily be filled through a managed service, professional service, or an on site vendor.

///

I will discuss the IT strategic theme alignment later in the chapter on strategic planning; for now, just take note of it. You may or may not have a strategic outcome alignment. This was our outcomes area designated by the budget process in Chattanooga.

So, looking at the example, we identified the gap in performance during the assessment. Then, we strategized a plan to fill the performance gap—and with success too. We exceeded the previous years' performance and beat our goal by 5%. You can do this with each of your core competencies to really see where you stand, plan how to fix it, and bring your performance up.

These are great tools to use not only in the strategic planning process, but also for budgeting. As I said earlier, Chattanooga uses the budgeting for outcomes method. Meaning, each year, we started over and used our performance metrics to justify our budget. This process encourages constant improvement, performance management, and ideally saving money in the long run.

We submitted our gap analysis along with our three-year strategic plan—really don't want to go beyond 3 years in tech, due to how fast it changes—plus our funding request, called an offer. That year we were at the top of the list for funding and didn't have any issues getting what we asked for. Everything was accounted for. Every dollar was tied to the strategic plan for its use. As we know, sometimes explaining IT to non-IT people who may not understand the need for what you are funding can be difficult, at best. This method makes it really easy for the folks deciding on your budget funding—in this case, what Chattanooga calls a results area team—to understand your plan and what you are doing. You can even describe why you need to do it. Just remember to keep it concise and clear. Think of the sections of this gap analysis form like a tweet; you are limited to a specific number of characters. This is by design, making it easier and quicker for you to do. Also, don't forget to understand your audience. No one wants to read a three-page explanation of why your customer service stinks. Summarize it and focus on fixing it.

Some of you may be thinking right now, "I don't want to highlight errors or problems in the department. We shouldn't have any gaps in service or elsewhere!" Sorry, but not true; and don't hide it. All it will do is make things worse for you and your IT group. Transparency is the key, and owning up to failures means you understand it and want to fix them. Refer back to our friend Fred in chapter one. Worrying about exposing flaws in his IT group is something he would do. But not you; you are a great CIO!

ENTERPRISE ARCHITECTURAL MODEL

Earlier I mentioned the enterprise architectural model (EAM); and it is asked as one of the assessment questions. So, what it is? And why you need it? It is precisely what its title states. A way to architect your enterprise technology and information systems.

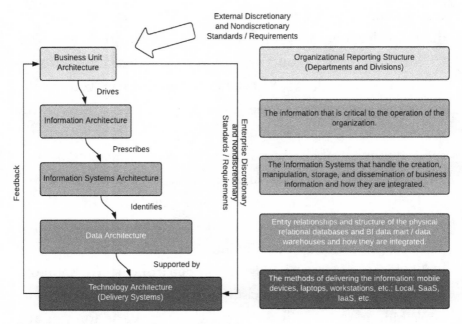

Figure 4-2: Enterprise Architectural Model

It's actually pretty simple when you look at it this way. The business unit architecture refers to the entire organization's reporting structure, including all departments and divisions. The EAM gives you an idea of how to think about data retrieval and storage later, driving the information architecture. This is the information critical to operating the organization, (e.g., court docket, traffic tickets, legal information, and so on), which then identifies the data architecture—starting to catch on? Here is where you identify your entity relationships, database structure, schemas, etc., and how they are integrated. All that is then supported by the technology architecture, otherwise known as the delivery systems. This is how both data and information is used and delivered to users (e.g., laptops, cloud systems, an ERP system, etc.)—yes, there is a difference between data and information. I know, you already know this and do it, because duh, every IT person knows that laptops use software to retrieve data from a database in a specified way to serve the users' business function. The problem with that line of thinking really shows itself when you are just winging it; asking what users want and not really putting much thought into why they want it, or even if they genuinely know why they want it.

Digging into the information architecture layer shows you flaws in business processes—yes, many business processes are flawed and typically not changed because…? Yup, you guessed it, it's the way they've always done it! I cringe, and a tiny part of me dies inside every time someone says that to me.

So, to summarize, a good assessment is absolutely critical to any strategic planning effort. Again if you don't know where you are, you will have no clue where you need to be or how to get there. And to summarize the enterprise architectural model, because you know how the organization is organized and works, you then know what to store/retrieve and why they store/retrieve it—how to structure the CRUD functions and how to integrate the systems. Now let's move on to getting organized and touch on formal governance.

CHAPTER FIVE

ORGANIZE AND GOVERN

"To rule is easy, to govern difficult." - Johann Wolfgang von Goethe

Great CIOs lead well-organized IT Groups with clear expectations, well-trained staff that understands IT's role and a clear vision of where they want technology in the organization, utilizing a formal IT Governance framework to help select and fund priority technology initiatives. They also embrace alternatives to traditional management and bureaucracy, such as Agile frameworks like Scrum and DevOps. On the contrary, poor CIOs are unorganized, despite thinking they are not; they have no vision. Their staff gets no direction; and they do not take the time to properly structure their IT group to provide the best value and build a great culture or govern IT initiatives.

GET ORGANIZED

When it comes to running an IT Group able to provide value

to the organization and its constituents, you need to be well organized. But what constitutes organized: federated, centralized, hybrid, or just do what your colleague has done with her IT Group? This is such a common question; but, there are no cookie-cutter methods that will work everywhere. The best way to organize is to constantly reorganize, based on your current strategy to best fulfill your vision, organizing an IT Group to best optimize IT resources for the organization and to add the most significant value, as efficiently possible. Great CIOs adapt. Just because they structured one IT group in City [A] one way doesn't mean the same structure will work in City [B]. You should continually evaluate and do what is best for your organization's structure, culture, and purpose. What method of organizing your IT Group will add the most significant value, be most efficient, and so on.

When it comes to the argument over federated or centralized IT groups, a centralized or a hybrid model works the best. This makes planning and governance much more straightforward and cost-effective. It also prevents turf wars and reduces or eliminates duplication of effort. The centralized IT Group keeps all IT resources in one central location under one set of policies and procedures. To the contrary, federated models, where each department has its own IT staff or even division, promote communication breakdowns, technology silos, segregated infrastructures, and many turf wars. It's the glorified official form of Shadow IT. Usually, when you have a bloke in department [A] who happens to have some IT skills because they took a college class or read a book. All of a sudden, they are assigned to do technology work in that department. Trust me, that never works out well and in some cases can even be a security risk.

A hybrid model is one where you keep most of the IT Group centralized, such as applications and project support, service desk, data center & data center support, security, and your IT operations. However, the hybrid part comes in when you have roaming or permanently assigned techs in specific departments with a higher need for direct critical or specialized support (e.g. police departments, fire departments, 911, 311, and radio communications sections). These techs will still report to a manager in the central IT Group.

Take a police department, for example. Let's say IT in a large municipality is a centralized department, covering perhaps five divisions. Applications: which handles the forward development for the organization, Infrastructure/Networking: which maintains the central datacenter and connected equipment, Operations: which oversees the day-to-day activities such as systems support and essentially keeping the ship afloat, Security: which is responsible for the disaster recovery planning, auditing of IT resources, and other such security-related tasks; and, finally Telecommunications, which handles IP and POTS type phone systems, radio systems, network cabling, etc. Within the Operations division may live a central Service Desk that takes incoming break/fix support calls and tracks them.

The Service Desk could have techs that could go out to various departments; or those techs could be assigned to the infrastructure/ networking division, etc. Some techs may be physically assigned to a specific department, such as Police, Fire-Rescue, or the Airport, and co-located on-site to provide immediate support for those specialized systems they may have expert knowledge of. However, they still report directly to the central IT Group. This is just one example of several possibilities. The service desk in a large organization, for example, may be a division all it's own; so, look at this example as one way to structure, not the definitive way to structure.

This example is how I first organized IT at the City of Chattanooga. Later, we changed to a DevOps and Agile structure, which is really the way to go for small to medium-sized IT groups in today's world. Again, your structure must evolve with the changes inside the organization and as better methods come about. Our department practically restructured every 18 months or so as we learned and grew with new IT methods, adapting to the organizational vision/mission. Sometimes we made giant leaps in change/reorganization; but, that's because we had to adapt and quickly. I can sum this up with a quote from W. Edwards Deming, *"It is not necessary to change. Survival is not mandatory."* Doesn't really get any clearer than that.

Great CIOs have a vision of the state they want IT to get to. Then they organize their department accordingly. They may shift resources and hire different roles as vacancies become available to best achieve their vision. They will specifically target focused specialties in most staff to meet the organizational goals. Also, they aren't afraid to take a talented firefighter with excellent development skills, learned independently without formal education, and hire and mentor them. There are hidden talents all over the organization. Find them; and, use them, especially those of you who have a small staff or have high budgetary restraints.

Poor CIOs don't really focus on an excellent organizational structure. They omit clear identification of roles, functional expertise scattered around different divisions, etc. And because these CIOs make no attempt to change anything, they always fill the positions with the same skillsets. "If it ain't broke, don't fix it" is the Status Quo CIOs' motto. They may keep systems running for decades beyond their expected end of life and fail to reevaluate their systems, service catalogs, or strategic goals—if they even have those. This translates into an organization that will need to one-day play catch-up and likely be a ripe target for ransomware attacks. These CIOs are also notorious for maintaining and servicing specific brands or systems, only worrying about a particular application rather than the service the system supports. For example, "we have always used system X as our email system. I know system Y can save us money or add functionality, but this is what we know and will always stick with."

The other portion of organizing your IT structure comes in the form of tools and processes, to be the most efficient you can be. Again, what really works best are agile methods, which allow flexibility in requirements gathering. For example, Scrum, one of the agile methodologies, works really well for IT groups who are heavy on the development side. DevOps works well for entire IT groups across any organization. All IT staff, regardless of functional specialty, should have some formal training in project management standards and agile principles. Suppose you are fortunate enough to have a large team with dedicated project managers or a Project Management Office (PMO). In that case, separating your functional groups from projects will be a little easier. If you work in a small environment with less staff, it becomes even more critical for you and your team to have a solid grasp of standard (waterfall) and, better (agile) project management best practices.

FORMAL GOVERNANCE

In the last chapter, we looked at the core competencies and why we assess them. One of those competencies—the first in fact—is governance. Whenever I speak of formal governance processes, I get odd looks. The most common misunderstanding is confusing governance with management. The two are not synonymous, in any way, and are actually two completely separate functions within the organization. In the traditional sense of the term, management refers to the control of inputs, outputs, and resources to successfully bring about a result. We manage human resources, technology, projects, operations, and a variety of other functions. Governance is more about controlling processes within an organization. The most widely understood example of governance is that of the "steering committee." However, I don't like using the term steering in the description of a formal governance process because it can become confusing to some who will look at it as a form of management.

Other examples of formal governance processes could be a strategic planning board, a project selection board, or even a single position in the organization called a capital projects planner. In IT, an excellent example of a formal governance process would be a board made up of each functional department head, chaired by either the CIO, Deputy CIO, or another chief executive such as a Deputy City Manager or Chief Operations Officer. The purpose of the board—let's call it the technology planning committee (TPC) in this example—is not to manage how to run the IT Group. That is the CIO's job. The board's purpose is to control how technology projects are selected, prioritized, and funded, which will tie into the regular budget process—hopefully outcomes/or performance-based.

Too many government organizations do not have a formal governance process in place. These organization's IT Groups are usually run by reactive order takers—like Fred. Remember, that the goal is to add value to the organization. That means that the organization's IT strategy must align with the organizational goals as best as possible, which means a formal governance process should be devised to aid the CIO in selecting the most beneficial IT projects for IT staff to work on.

Digging into the technology planning committee example, ideally, this committee should meet quarterly. Still, it could also only meet toward the beginning of a budget cycle when capital planning is in full swing. Whatever time frame works best for your organization, but for best results, the committee should meet at least twice a year if you use this basic governance example. One of this committee's primary responsibilities is to examine business cases, feasibility studies, and the like for impact on the organization, selection, prioritization, and funding of capital technology-related projects. This serves several valuable purposes. It is an excellent way to prevent duplication of effort, which is especially important in organizations still using a federated IT organizational model. It encourages open communication among all functional department heads and provides a central forum to demonstrate how the potential technology project will impact the entire organization or how it won't. It also offers a formal mechanism for grant funding, or when going before an elected board like a City Council or County Commission for approval.

Okay, I know, I know—the terms and functions of a committee in government? Whoah! I know what you are thinking but hear me out. Yes, a committee can be complex and cause further complications depending on the organization: who is in charge, how its organized, and who it reports to. I've been there, done that, and got the T-shirt. I understand that is scary. And some of you may have experienced some pretty horrible committee experiences. This example is just one you will have to judge for yourself in your organization. That said, it can and does provide you with some assurances and priorities. Meaning it's not left up to the CIO to take EVERY capital request for technology in at one time and decide him or herself what should take priority and what should go first, then next. It puts all department heads and decision-makers in one room to clarify and decide what a priority for funding is. This means you have a clear set of expectations with no ambiguous or unrealistic viewpoints of what will happen. It also helps all the other departments that demand their technology project take priority over others, due to the fact, they participate enough to not get all up in your face about their project when working on Department A's project first—assuming you have only staff for one or a few at a time. In order to decide what business cases need to go before the committee, all technology project proposals could be evaluated on some sort of scale, like the following sample point system scale—but this is just one simple example to drive home the concept:

Organizational impact (How does this affect the organization as a whole, if at all)

Low - 1 - 2 - 3 - 4 - 5 - High

One Division - Entire Organization

Project Resource Hours (Estimated amount of time where resources will need to be involved)

Low - 1 - 2 - 3 - 4 - 5 - High

Less than 1 FTE Hour - Greater than 480 FTE hours

Projected Costs (How much will need to be budgeted. Include all resources and equipment)
<u>**Low - 1 - 2 - 3 - 4 - 5 - High**</u>
Less than $3,000 - Greater than $50,000

IT Impact (How will IT staff be involved, how many IT personnel required)
<u>**Low - 1 - 2 - 3 - 4 - 5 - High**</u>
Vendor only support - 3 or more IT FTE required

Mandated by Law (Is it required by law in some way? e.g., HIPAA, ADA, etc.)
<u>**Low - 1 - 2 - 3 - 4 - 5 - High**</u>
No Mandates - Mandatory

TOTAL points possible: **25**

In this simple example, project proposals with a score of 12 or higher, or lower than 12 total but high organization impact, must go before the committee (TPC) to be reviewed and approved. Anything less than a score of 12 could be sent to the CIO or designee to determine if it should go before the committee. This includes project proposals from IT and all other business cost or revenue centers with a significant technology component. The criteria are really up to what the organization deems appropriate to get the most value from the governance committee. As the CIO, you should be at the table driving the initiative to help your IT Group succeed in your organization. And keep in mind all these measures can be customized to your organization.

To see this example in action. Let's look at this sample case. Say that Roberta, an Economic Development Manager of Metro City, went to a conference and came back with an idea to solve a big problem her department has been faced with for some time. The product she discovered costs just over 100,000 dollars. However, as she describes the awesome demonstration and conversation she had with the vendor at the conference booth, she says it is more than worth it. In an organization without a formal IT governance process in place, this may get funded through any number of means, or worse, might be implemented without IT even being involved or aware; and, as a result, it will likely be siloed from other information systems or not configured well for maximum value. Worse yet it could be started then abandoned.

Perhaps they decided afterward that the system wasn't a solution for the real problem, but only caused more issues they could not have foreseen without some technology expertise. Or, maybe it does work well; but, the other part of the project required for it to integrate with other systems didn't get funded. Now the municipality is stuck with a piece of software that taxpayers have spent $100,000 on, and no one uses it. I have, unfortunately, seen that happen with multi-million dollar systems.

Another example is one organization that spent 1.3 Million dollars on a sophisticated CRM (customer resource management) system without thinking first of how the system would actually be used and by whom. That project went on for two years and half of what was needed was never even funded up front. This led to the entire system being scrapped and all that money wasted. Simply put, the agency was looking to implement 311 software to track requests coming in from constituents, but didn't bother to actually fund and create a 311 call center to use it. Instead they tried to get all departments to use it—huge flop. That is what IT Governance is for, to help mitigate these situations and reduce the load and stress on you, your IT group, and potentially save the organization time and money.

Continuing with our sample case, let's say Roberta happens to work for a municipality with a simple IT governance process. She writes up a strong business case complete with financial analysis and feasibility study and scores the proposal against the Technology Planning Committee scale example. The organizational impact is a 4. It will affect most areas of the organization but not all areas. Project resource hours are a 3, since the vendor will do most of the work. However, some City resources will also need to be involved throughout the project schedule. Projected costs are 5; they are greater than $50,000. The IT impact she is told will be a 2. And, since the system is not mandated by law, it receives a score of 1 for that item. The total score is 15, which is above the required score of 12 to require the proposal to be approved by the Technology Planning Committee. Roberta sends the proposal over to the committee chair and gets it on the agenda for the next meeting. At the meeting, she presents her business case in detail, and the committee members discuss the proposal. Seeing the value in her submission, the committee approves the proposal. The total project costs are then included in the next year's capital budget and tracked throughout the project. This simple method also ties in nicely with and can be adapted for performance or outcomes-based budgeting models.

This is just a basic case example. Some organizations require all project proposals to go before a governance committee of some kind, regardless of a scoring mechanism. Even though this method may be partially subjective, the positive side of using a scoring tool like this one, is the mechanism requires the person making the proposal to really think about the impact the project's outcome will have on the entire organization. All too often, this seemingly obvious thought does not happen. People just see something they want, without any idea about how it will work in their organization. Will it even work at all? Are the risk factors too high? Is it cost-prohibitive? What resources are really involved in doing this, etc.? It ends up being implemented and, in some cases, eventually abandoned—as in the previously mentioned 311 example. It is up to you and your organization to decide the best IT governance method that is most efficient and effective for your organization.

Feel free to use the example scoring method provided here as a starting point. This simple example is designed to be quickly implemented, explained, and use specifically for government organizations just starting off with IT governance. Some organizations choose to implement a standard framework for governing IT in the organization, such as ISACA's COBIT—as of this writing now in version 2019. This is a good practice that gets the entire organization involved in the governance process. Other organizations have taken on outcomes-based budgeting (e.g. budgeting for outcomes) or performance-based budgeting similar to the methods private and nonprofit organizations have used for years. I highly recommend a performance-based budgeting model of some kind, with a formal strategy and management system like the balanced scorecard or some other outcomes-based model. It is efficient and shows the significance of a real, measurable value, even when dealing with intangible things like IT.

When the entire organization has a solid outcomes-based budgeting process, IT governance can, and should, be incorporated in the process. For example, any offer containing any technology component that could be funded, should then go before the technology planning committee to prioritize each offer, as I previously described. If performed correctly, some offers may not end up being funded that year allowing the capitol funds to be better allocated.

In many of the other public sector agencies I researched, there was no governance model, because the CIO feared that their department would be run by a committee—somehow losing their status and power. Remember, the point of a formal IT governance process is to enhance IT's value, not run the IT Group. IT Governance models should not be designed to run the functional aspects of IT. Meaning, management is a separate practice from governance. In its simplest form, IT governance is an IT initiative selection and priority tool that helps ensure that the initiatives—projects—your IT staff work on are all funded, prioritized, and aligned with the organization's mission.

Some CIOs take on way too much and don't know how to say NO, let alone set the priority. That's where IT governance can help. A friend and IT colleague of mine once said in one of our planning meetings, "*Everything can't be a priority. If everything is a priority, then nothing is.*" By setting the priority and order of technology projects and basing the level of work on the IT group's resources and capabilities, you ensure the essential, most strategically valuable items get funded and accomplished first. Without some form of governance, whether a simple system like the example in this book, or a more elaborate and advanced system based on the COBIT framework, you and your staff are set up to waste a great deal of effort, time, and money. Some CIOs have told me that they didn't need a committee to tell them which projects they need to work on—mostly opting to do all them and all at once. Sadly this attitude toward governance practices means that those CIOs and their staff waste a great deal of time, effort, and money easily avoided by applying even a simple governance process.

CHAPTER SIX
BUILD PARTNERSHIPS

❝ *If you can't explain it simply, you don't understand it well enough."* ~Albert Einstein

❝ *Tell me and I forget. Teach me and I remember. Involve me and I learn."* ~Benjamin Franklin

What is IT? How is IT valuable to the organization? Is all IT the same? Amazingly enough, you would be surprised about how many public sector CIOs can't answer these seemingly simple questions. In all honesty, many chief executives want to know what IT can do to achieve their vision; they may not care outside of that. Again, we come to the repeating theme of this book: value. What value can IT provide the organization? When I asked several CIOs how that statement plays out in their organization, the answer varied slightly. Still, the premise was, the "what value" is the chief executive and other department executives' concern. The "how value" is the concern of the CIO. When I asked CIOs if their chief executives understood what IT was, the result was a predictable no. I then asked if the CIO had bothered to explain what IT was at any point. What purpose does IT serve in the organization? What is the role of IT? Again, the answer was, essentially no. In some cases, there was confusion as to why that was even important.

Often, CIOs assume that the chief executives know what IT is and the purpose. You may be surprised to find out that is not always the case, especially in the public sector. And, those chief executives—or your peer department heads—who do claim to understand, might have the wrong impression. A lot of the time, the perception is that IT is no different than Fleet Management. IT procures, maintains, fixes, inventories, and retires computer and telecommunications equipment, much like Fleet Management would do with the organization's vehicle fleet. One executive of a large metropolitan city in the United States put it to me like this, "If I need a car for a trip to an out-of-town meeting, I go to Fleet. If I want to hire someone, I go to HR. If I need a new computer on my desk or a laptop for my trip, I go to IT. It's that simple." This misconception of what IT is and the value that IT creates for the organization is a critical factor in the success or failure of an organizational IT program, and part of the CIO's role is to define that value and frequently reiterate that value—did I mention frequently? It is essential to define and clarify IT's role and importance to the organization's top executives gaining their support and respect—internal marketing, if you will. There are those public CIOs out there who do report directly to the chief executive. Other CIOs may report to the deputy chief executive. Others may report to the CFO, an old-fashioned and obsolete reporting structure due to the IT function getting a start in the first digital financial systems. Still, others report to places in the organizational structure you might not have ever imagined. I have even seen a large municipality whose CIO reported directly to the chief executive, but the CIO didn't run any IT operational functions. A different functional executive actually ran the IT Group. That person was titled the IT COO (Chief Operating Officer) who reported to a different department director who reported to the chief executive. This organization is a little confusing and has several silos for communications, information, and data. There have been, and probably will continue to be, countless debates on the best place for a CIO to report in an organization—both in the public and private sector. These debates are sometimes driven by ego more so than logic; but, nonetheless, they exist.

In most cases, regardless of the organizational reporting structure, the most common complaint among strategic CIOs is that they don't feel they have an adequate role in the organization or are sometimes referred to as an adequate "seat at the planning table." In reality, who the CIO reports to is not that critical if there are open lines of communication across all senior executives. However, it is critical for the CIO to have a seat at the proverbial planning table. The CIO must be intimately involved in the organizational leadership and planning, just as any other department head would.

The reasons go back to IT's value, or rather the value IT brings to the organization. Great CIOs will, of course, take full advantage of every opportunity to market the value of IT to the organization as a partner, not just another internal vendor at the organization's beck and call.

To achieve a seat at the so-called planning table, the value-driven CIO must define their role in the organization, then explain IT's role in plain business terms the chief executive and other department executives who may not be tech-savvy, can understand. This business acumen is a critical skill for any modern value-driven CIO's modus operandi. Explaining the value IT has in achieving the organizational mission and vision will lead to the crucial component of partnering with other departments. I cannot emphasize enough, how important it is to partner with your colleagues if you want them to take you seriously, and give you the respect that so many reactive CIOs think should be automatically given, and not earned. If the IT group is not understood and chooses not to partner, you will most likely find it hard to be taken seriously or included in critical business planning.

Becoming a partner with your colleagues is also vital for another reason. How many times have you heard someone in the IT Group use the phrase "helping our customers" or "...our users?" You may have even said it yourself a time or two. Have you ever stopped to think about the terms customers and users and what they mean to IT? When I ask this question, I always get a bewildered look. The answer is usually something like, "our customers are our users," or "we support the departments inside the organization, so they are our customers." or, "we have internal customers only." I half expect to hear "duh!" mumbled under the breath of the person answering my seemingly silly inquiry. Perhaps you just chuckled at this question, as well. Okay, fair enough. A long time ago, I looked at things the same way. So I can understand why that question may sound strange. Bare with me for a bit. I promise I can change your mind about how you view your "customers."

By definition, in any organization, the customer is the recipient of the end product or service the organization provides. In the case of a local municipality, 99.99% of the time, the customer is the citizen and business taxpayers. So, who are the actual customers of IT then? That is a trick question. The answer is the same customer of the Police Department, Public Works, Parks, Transportation, and other such public-facing departments have, the taxpaying constituents and visitors to your area. IT's relationship to the customer is not direct in most cases, which may be why this concept is not easy for the reactive-minded CIO to comprehend. IT "partners" with the other departments in the organization, who in turn directly deal with the customer. However, I have seen a few IT Groups who directly serve and interact with customers in increasingly growing numbers—especially in very large agencies with hundreds of IT staff. This concept is the same for IT, in any organization, public or private sector. If you treat your colleagues as customers, lined up in front of a menu board and a cash register, then you will be treated as a vendor, who is expected to deliver on command. Serving at the other departments' pleasure, instead of a partner at the planning table, who has a critical role in the organizational strategy. Remember, IT should not just be taking requests or orders from other departments. That is reactive behavior; and, a reactive state of mind is not where the organization needs its CIO to be. CIOs who happen to be reactive order takers are the ones who can't comprehend the concept, business unit leaders might not understand what IT is, or what value IT has in the organization.

Here are a few tips you can use to partner with the business units and gain insight into the regular operations:

GO TO THE GEMBA.

Learn about as many functions in your organization as you can. The Japanese have a term appropriate for describing this: Gemba, meaning the real place. Go and see the operations with your staff. Explore how your partners use technology in their daily activities. Don't just do it once and never do it again either. Every few years, technology changes, processes change, and people come and go. These changes bring new ways of doing things. Change can always be counted on. Embrace change and plan for it. There is no better way to do this than going to the Gemba. This action not only gives you exposure to the rest of the organization, but this exposure is a building block in forming trust and relationships (i.e. partnerships). Be a catalyst for change and go to the Gemba.

An example of this is what we did in Chattanooga. We sent our entire DevOps team to embed themselves into our Police department during some very critical projects. The results were a team that saw first hand what was going on and how to solve the issues related to the creation of Chattanooga's Real-Time Intelligence Center (RTIC).

MEET WITH YOUR PARTNERS REGULARLY.

The best approach to meeting and discussing technology-related strategy and planning is through a formal governance committee for IT, as discussed in chapter 5. However, a regularly scheduled meeting between you, your IT Management staff, your partners, and their management staff will work wonders for building trusting relationships. Also, it helps you to get the information you need to formulate a strategy for the organization's technology. More work is involved because part of your agenda should include discussing technology-related initiatives in other functional areas, which may impact the partner you are meeting with. Needless to say, it is worth the extra effort. You should regularly take a roll call, perhaps with a sign-in sheet, and have a meeting agenda. It is sometimes helpful to send back the key points of information you collected to the attendees, to confirm the discussion's critical points. Also, you should not just focus their discussion on technology-related issues. Encourage them to talk about the pain points they face every day, especially in your first few meetings. This way, you will learn more than if you try to describe just the technology they need. Remember, they may not be tech-savvy and may not even realize that there could be a technology solution to a problem they face. There is also aways the chance technology may not be the answer.

Anyone who has ever used agile methodologies acknowledges that most of the time, folks don't know what they want until they see it in action. You can always sift through what they tell you for nuggets where the technology may help add value, save costs, or make procedures more efficient. Always be upbeat and positive in these meetings. Be honest and open, but try not to point fingers or blame for procedural mishaps and the like. These tend to put people off. And you will lose your momentum, not to mention maybe some cool points too.

Also, take responsibility for your department's shortcomings and be direct about them. Your partners will respect you far more for being honest and taking responsibility than trying to hide or push off the blame. Especially where a failed project or procedure is concerned and the IT group dropped the ball. Although not required, another good tip is to meet your partners on their turf. Depending on the person, if you constantly make them drive across town or even walk across the street to meet with you, you can sometimes put them on guard. If they are on their turf, people will likely open up more and accept the process. This concept also goes back to tip one, going to the Gemba.

Once you have met with all organization areas, mine the information you collected, look for patterns and anomalies. This is mostly for your benefit, however, you could combine your findings into a single short report you can share with all your partners. The report does a few things for your partners. It shows them that you are reaffirming you heard their issues, confirming they didn't throw their issues into a big void. Furthermore, it provides each area or department with a view of other areas and departments' issues and correlates it with IT. It can show the commonalities you are trying to find and reduce potential duplication of efforts. This information will later be used as fuel for your strategy.

Don't wait for a less busy time to interact with your partners.

How many times have you put something off because of other priorities or projects? We have all done it at least a few times in our careers. Interacting with your partners face-to-face, even if it's Zoom, should be the highest priority and scheduled at a minimum of every quarter. I find scheduling monthly meetings means you meet about every two to three months due to scheduling conflicts. When new department heads come on board, don't wait for the next chief executive's meeting, or whatever your organization calls it, to get the typically quick how-do-you-do and welcome to you introduction of the new department head by your chief executive. You should make an appointment to introduce yourself and meet the new department head within the first weeks of their arrival.

You will know when that is, after all, because your department will, of course, create their network accounts and the like. There is no need to talk shop for a long time. You just want to do a quick meet and greet. Explain your role in the organization and learn a little about your new partner, establishing a good working relationship with your new partner early on. This gives you a foundation for creating a [hopefully] long-lasting partnership with someone who will inevitably have a different philosophy and strategy than their predecessor did. This means that your strategy may also need to adjust accordingly.

To best start this partnering process, you need to explain the concept of partner vs. customer to your staff, and when possible, make it a part of the organization's paradigm and culture. Help your team understand the concept and repeat it often. Using the term partner, instead of customer, is not enough by itself. You need to go out physically and partner with the other departments. Talk, engage, and take every opportunity to learn about potential areas where IT can add value to your partners and the organization. That includes transcending the standard expected service delivery from IT by partnering on other special projects, supporting your partner's initiatives, and so on. Doing this is always easiest when the organization has a straightforward strategic planning process with official objectives and initiatives with real valuable metrics and key performance indicators (KPIs). Some form of formal governance for IT is also essential. If your organization doesn't have a formal IT governance process of some kind, then now is the perfect time to create one. Even the simplest governance mechanism can have substantial lasting effects on the value of IT. And if your organization doesn't have some KPI-based performance measuring program or outcomes-based budgeting process, that doesn't mean you shouldn't measure things in your department. Pave the way. Set the standard. Create value!

CHAPTER SEVEN
YOUR MISSION

❝ *You can't steal second base and keep one foot on first."*
~ Frederick B. Wilson

Your mission and vision statements are imperative starting points in strategic planning, even in the public sector, where it seems the mission never changes. Furthermore, they also serve the purpose of increasing morale and direction in your staff. There are some very subtle differences between mission and vision statements in the private sector and the public sector. There are also differences in how these statements are written between an entire organization and just one department/division within that organization. Think of the vision statement as a way to summarize where you want to be. The mission statement is the what, how, and for whom you do what you do to get there.

The vision statement rarely, if ever, changes, at least in the private sector, but the mission statement may change as needed from time to time. A government organization or agency's mission or vision may vary due to chief executives coming and going, each with a different vision for achieving their organizational mission. Mission and vision statements can and should be used at low levels of an organization. For example, I encourage my staff to establish and write mission statements for programs or projects. Regardless, the mission and vision statements are the starting point for any strategy at all organizational levels. It is what you as a CIO should use to guide your IT Group. Set a vision for technology used by the organization and define your staff's mission, allowing them to know where to go and how to get there. The best mission and vision statements are clear, concise, and memorable. They shouldn't be more than three sentences maximum and can be as short as a single word if one can find a word, to sum up their entire mission or vision. To be impactful and inspiring, it should be as short and memorable as possible.

The Mission Statement

Your mission, should you choose to accept it… Don't worry, this book won't explode. Your head might from reading it, but the book itself is inherently safe, for the most part.

The organizational mission statement is the concise definition of the purpose of the organization. The mission statement must answer two questions very succinctly:

1. What does the organization do?
2. How does the organization do what it does?

Easy right? Private sector companies and nonprofit's mission statements will also answer a third question: the organization's customer base or market segment. In the public sector, the customer base is always the same, so it is acceptable to leave it out. Though, including terms like "citizens," "taxpayers," "tourists," and the like aren't uncommon in public sector mission statements.

Let's take a look at an example mission statement courtesy of a sunny city in the Southern United States:

"We are committed to providing excellent public service and safety to all who live, work, and play in our vibrant, tropical, historic community."

The first thing that jumps out about this mission statement is the use of personal pronouns, in this case, "we." Mission and vision statements should not contain "I," "we." "us," or "our," anywhere in the statement. However, personal pronouns can be used in value statements, sometimes called an operating philosophy. Does the statement accurately reflect what the City does and how they do it? Yes, "…Providing excellent public service and safety…" to the citizens and visitors describes what the City does. However, the statement doesn't demonstrate how the City will provide this excellent service and safety to its citizens and visitors. Thus, it doesn't pass the two-question test. The statement does support the third question of whom the City serves. Still, again, this is optional information for a government organization because it is assumed the organization will serve all residents and visitors to the area. In other words, there is no target market segment. What is more important is how the City provides excellent public service. Something measurable is even better.

THE CIO's MISSION FOR IT

Your department's mission eloquently put into words to form your mission statement is the absolute acme of your strategy. Your mission statement is your IT Group's succinct definition; it is your purpose and the embodiment of what you do for the organization. Like the organizational mission statement, the IT Group mission statement answers the same two questions very succinctly.

1. What does the IT Group do for the organization?
2. How does the IT Group do what it does for the organization?

Here is an example of an IT mission statement I wrote for the City of Chattanooga, Tennessee's IT Group, when I came on board as their CIO:

"To serve as the catalyst for digital transformation and innovation."

This isn't just a random clustering of buzzwords to form a statement that sounds really neat. The City of Chattanooga was in the beginning stages of moving to a Budgeting for Outcomes (BFO) model. The mayor at that time, Andy Berke, had five distinct outcome areas that he wanted us to focus on to transform the City operations:

1. Safer Streets,
2. A growing Economy,
3. Stronger Neighborhoods,
4. Smarter Students & Stronger Families,
5. High Performing Government (Efficient and Innovative),

The mission of the IT Group has to support the mission of the organization—be in alignment. In the case with Chattanooga, the IT Group had to directly support the 5th results area, High Performing Government, and the other four results areas indirectly through service to our partner departments throughout the City, and ultimately the City's customers and constituents. The mission statement also aligns with the organization's open government objectives, continuing to be a distinct and highly innovative community. Let's break down the mission statement and put it against the two rule criteria.

What we [IT] do, "...a catalyst for digital transformation and innovation..." and why. It ties in with the organization's mission. Being a catalyst and enabling digital transformation and innovation leads to higher performing government tying in with the other four outcome areas. This mission statement passes the formulation criteria just fine. It's also short and simple, which means it is easy to remember. So, if you haven't already, craft, or revamp, your mission statement to help explain what IT does for your organization and why. Your mission statement not only drives your vision; but it drives your entire department and staff. Take every opportunity you can to reaffirm your department's mission to your team. Be it through a staff meeting, a one-on-one chat in the hallway, project kickoff, etc., your staff is more effective when they know why they are working (i.e. mission) and what they are working toward (i.e. vision). Having a leader reaffirm their purpose, the department's mission and vision will also strengthen esprit de corps in your department, which can also have a daisy chain effect elsewhere in the organization through bottom-up and lateral leadership.

SHORT, INSPIRING, AND UNFORGETTABLE

No, I'm not referring to someone's online dating ad. I am referring to the traits of some of the best mission statements I've ever read. These highly memorable mission statements from world-renowned nonprofits and public sector agencies are short inspiring messages that encapsulate the very essence of each organization's purpose in twenty-eight words or less. Can you do the same for your IT Group or organization?

TED

"Spreading Ideas."

The New York City Public Library

"To inspire lifelong learning, advance knowledge, and strengthen our communities."

National Public Radio (NPR)

"To work in partnership with member stations to create a more informed public – one challenged and invigorated by a deeper understanding and appreciation of events, ideas, and cultures."

American Red Cross

"Prevents and alleviates human suffering in the face of emergencies by mobilizing the power of volunteers and the generosity of donors."

Public Broadcasting System (PBS)

"To create content that educates, informs, and inspires."

The Smithsonian Institute

"The increase and diffusion of knowledge."

Let these few statements of the public sector and not-for-profit organizations worldwide inspire you to create a short and memorable mission statement for your organization, department, division, or team.

THE VISION STATEMENT

Did you know when you got into this business that you would have to look into the future? We don't have magic crystal balls to give us a vision of the future state of technology. So, the CIO needs to be a visionary or at the very least listen to her staff, who may be visionaries. For the organization itself, the vision statement is the ultimate objective(s) for the organization (i.e. where the organization is going and where or what it wants to be). It conveys purpose and values and should inspire the organization's employees to share in that vision and work toward it. The vision statement only answers a single question: where do you want to be in the future?

Ideally, your vision statement should be hopeful and inspiring. I've heard stories of people wanting to join an organization simply because they have a similar vision for the organization's future. The organization's vision statement inspired these people to come work for them. That's what your vision statement should be—

inspiring.

In the private sector, the vision statement is usually the founder's vision of what the company was created to do. In the public sector, the vision statement is a bit different. The vision statement for a local government's chief executive should be a clear, concise statement about a realistic future state, as well as the role the organization will play in that state. It should be inspiring and even striving for perfection, even though perfection is not achievable. The constant change and adaptation the organization takes to better itself toward that vision is worth the efforts. Take this example from a medium-sized U.S. Municipal Police Department.

"To eliminate crime and become the safest community in the country."

Short, sweet, and with impact. Though the elimination of crime is impossible, the police department could help the community to become the country's safest community. The Chief of Police for this City has the vision to inspire her officers to go out and proactively make the City's streets the safest in the nation. The vision statement is something inspiring for every police officer in that community to think about when they go out on patrol. Here is another example:

"The single most livable, safe and prosperous community in America."

Like the first example, this vision statement is definitely validly composed; it has direction, is clear and concise. It is motivating and maybe pie-high-in-the-sky, but it sure is worth the effort needed to achieve. Here is another example:

> *"The City of XXXXXX will be a model of excellence that puts citizens first. Skilled motivated employees will be known for providing quality and value in all areas of service. We will be a platform for vital economic activity that gives XXXXXX a competitive edge in the marketplace. We will partner with citizens and businesses to make this a community of choice for living, working and leisure activities."*

This is a realistic vision statement that can be used as a primary motivational mechanism for staff. "A model of excellence," "Putting citizens first," "Motivated employees...known for... quality and value..." These are all positively motivating statements well within reach and clear enough for each department in the City to use in planning a strategy to help achieve that vision. The only caveat is that it is a bit long. It's harder to be memorable and have an impact when the vision statement is several sentences. That said, it is still a valid statement to strive for.

The CIO Vision for IT

If you are wondering why I used non-IT-related vision statements to establish a section on the CIO's vision, it is because, like with the mission statement, IT's value to the organization must be as a part of the organization, sharing in and supporting the organizational vision—alignment. If IT's vision was heading in the opposite direction, or IT didn't have a good vision, or worse yet had no vision at all, then what value do you suppose IT would be providing the organization? Not a whole lot. Here is one of my favorite quotes: "*Vision without action is a daydream. Action without vision is a nightmare.*" I use this quote in many of the lectures and classes I've taught over the years. It sums up the concept I teach about being reactive vs. proactive very nicely. Literally, those CIOs with no vision of where their IT Group and the organization need to be in the coming years, just take action. The staff who work for such a CIO subsequently live in a nightmare with no direction, clear objectives, nothing measured and not much accomplished. I have seen and experienced this situation first hand, and it is not pretty. These IT groups are constantly reactive, taking and fulfilling orders, no different from a fast-food restaurant. That is "action without vision"—a nightmare.

Let me be clear. There is always some element of reactivity to an IT Group. It's the nature of the beast. How you deal with that demand, organize and channel the demand, separates the great CIOs from the poorest ones. After all, luck favors the prepared. On the contrary, CIOs who talk the talk, have great ideas, and a clear vision, but for whatever reason don't ever take any action beyond the status quo live in a daydream. That is "vision without action." Fear may stop them from venturing out, perhaps? Your guess is as good a mine as to why. But my advice to these CIOs is, nothing ventured, nothing gained so get a move on.

Great CIOs have a clear vision of the future state they want their department to be in as well as the state they want the organization to be in. They share the vision with their staff and the rest of the organization, then partner with their peers to see the vision through to fruition. That is vision with action; and that is the state you want your organization and IT Group to be in. A vision statement for an individual department within the organization, such as your IT Group, should reflect on the vision for the organization but still be somewhat unique to your vision for IT. Using the last City example, the IT Group for that City may write a vision statement like this one:

"The IT Group for the City of XXXXXXX will be a model of excellence that through highly skilled and motivated employees will be known for providing quality technology services and products while creating and sustaining value in information systems and technology throughout the City's business units."

Another example is the vision statement I wrote for IT as the CIO for the City of Chattanooga, TN.

"To be a value-driven steward of information systems and innovation for the City of Chattanooga."

Feel free to use my examples as a starting point or copy it and use as is. But remember, just because you wrote, or copied, a vision statement and passed it out to your staff does not mean you now have a vision, allowing you to go on about your business as usual. The vision needs to be authentic. And you must sell that vision to your staff and the organization. You must strive to achieve the vision by completing the rest of the strategic planning process and see the vision through to fruition.

Another question I always get asked going through the portion on writing vision statements is, "so what do we do when we have achieved our mission?" The answer is simple, you sustain it or create a new mission based on the organization's ever-changing direction. The world we live in is a dynamic world and is constantly in a state of change. You must be adaptive and change to survive. However, merely surviving is not enough as far as I am concerned. I suggest being a catalyst for change, go forth and innovate, make mistakes, and learn. Change is going to happen regardless if you want it to or not, so you might as well embrace and even guide change to make it happen when it needs to. And this is the basis for developing your strategy and achieve your vision.

CHAPTER EIGHT
STRATEGY

❝_Planning is bringing the future into the present so that you can do something about it now._" *~Alan Lakein*

In chapter four I discussed the importance of getting a good assessment of your IT group and organization to plan appropriately. Now it's time to pull out those gap analyses and start planning your strategy. But, what do I mean by strategic planning? If you have ever flipped through your contacts in LinkedIn, you may have noticed a common skill listed in near every profile regardless of industry: strategic planning.

Curiously, a great deal of the people I asked may be able to define strategic planning or strategic thinking, but don't actually think strategically. Instead, they think operationally and call it a strategy. This, unfortunately, is especially true in the public sector. John Luthy, Ph.D., the founder and president of The Futures Corporation and managing director of the Executive Management Development Institute, indicates that public-sector strategic plans have become skewed toward operations plans. Only about 15% of the plan is actually strategic. The remaining 85% is operational and action-centric. So, what do you think of when you think of a strategic plan?

Let's briefly go back to Fred from chapter one. Fred would say that because of the amount of work being requested of his IT group, over six years' worth of work, there would be no need to look past the next few months. His staff just needed to finish the projects currently on their plate checking them off his master to-do list. More work will keep coming in. And they will still need to do it. The requests will never stop. Fred's idea of a strategic plan is meeting his customer's needs exactly, assuring all the projects get done—that means not questioning anything even if it brings up questions. Fred would say, "this project checklist right here is all the strategy we need." In actuality, that is a horrible plan and not even a strategy. For starters, not questioning anything and always being told what to do for the organization causes several problems. The most glaring is it puts your IT group firmly in a reactive state and means your partners aren't looking at you as a partner but rather more like they would a vendor—discussed in chapter six. They come to expect you are there to please them and do what they say rather than partner with them and work together for the betterment of the organization as a whole. And second, it means you will end up working on a lot of unfunded projects. Projects that may not get finished or get stopped mid-way through. You will have disparate systems all over your organization that make performance management difficult, if not impossible. Once again, I quote the great author, Alan Lakein:

"failing to plan is planning to fail."

There is a great deal more to strategic planning for IT than just checking off a list of projects the organization requests of IT. That is a clear indicator the CIO has no vision or any thought of the future state of things in his organization. I cannot stress enough how important having a sound vision of IT's future state in an organization is to a CIO. Without it, there can be no real strategic planning. There are countless business books and executives in all kinds of organizations who will stress the same importance of having a vision—go read Alan Lakein's books. I once had a debate with a CIO who worked for a religion-based university on the importance of having a vision, and was disappointed the CIO disagreed with me. I explained even the Bible mentions the necessity for vision. *"Where there is no vision, the people perish."* — Proverbs 29:18. I can assure you this CIO's staff were definitely perishing, and the faculty, staff, and students of the university suffered for it.

I was speaking at a conference about leadership one spring. A gentleman from a rather large municipality came up to me after my session. He spoke candidly about his experience with his CIO and how he was interested in making a difference. Still, it was difficult without proper leadership and direction. He put it to me like this:

"Because we have no strategy, no direction, no feedback, and no vision, we are just the purveyors of a reactive list of things to do and check off, we [staff] are essentially like Smokejumpers. Ferried

to a forest fire and dropped into the middle of the fire, instantly surrounded by numerous risks that could kill you and forced to fight our way out from the inside. That is how we get assigned and manage projects and service requests in this department. And with no thought on the impact of the work performed, no measurement of the outcomes, no alignment with the budget, no vision of purpose, and the high probability that two months into the project, it could be killed off for who knows what reason. IT Smokejumpers, that's what we are! And as such, we have to fend for ourselves, fighting for resources, isolated and cut off from the rest of the organization, and just hoping the CIO doesn't toss any heavy objects on us or push us into the flames to protect himself while we fight our project fires."

That is quite a powerful statement. I advised, he can't change his CIO and shouldn't try to. If he was passionate about what he was doing, then to try and lead from his position, lead up. And, be a leader to his peers and his staff. Show his team what good leadership is and try to isolate them from the CIO's negativity as much as possible. Or, move on somewhere else and away from that CIO. I also spoke to this manager's CIO later in the day. The CIO felt his staff were happy, productive, motivated and insisted his staff thought highly of him as a respected leader in the organization and community. *"They all look up to me as a leader... they all know I mean business and not to question my authority,"* he stated to me. Obviously, the opposite was true. He was totally blind to reality and his staff's true feelings. And his authoritarian mindset was not helping matters either. His staff just treated him like the emperor with no clothes on. The municipality he worked for and the citizens of his community all suffered as a result.

WHAT IS STRATEGIC PLANNING?

The formal definition of strategic planning "…is the process by which the guiding members of an organization envision its future and develop the necessary procedures and operations to achieve that future." The definition refers to the "guiding members of an organization." In the traditional sense of strategy and leadership, the guidance came from the top and trickled down to the front-line workers. That is not always the case anymore, especially in the public sector. It is not uncommon for strategy and leadership to come from all areas of the organization. There is another key element to this definition: "…envision its future…" You guessed it, you can't have a strategic plan without knowing where you want to go (i.e. having a vision). Ironically, this is the tricky part for some CIOs to understand. Usually, these CIOs make the incorrect assumption that their organization and everyone automatically knows the IT group's purpose, as well as, what role the CIO should take. Subsequently, they don't spend enough time strategizing technology for the organization; or, if they do, they don't spend enough time marketing their strategy to their partners. Sometimes, their strategy is entirely focused solely on the IT group and not the organization as a whole. As CIO, your purpose for strategic planning in IT is to enact a digital transformation and innovate the organization's business goals with technology to help achieve the organizational mission and vision—add value to the organization.

The actual activity of strategic planning itself is mostly an iterative process. Thus, it can be started at any point in the cycle, but usually follows a formal beginning or entry point, especially by organizations who do not currently have a formal strategic planning process in place. For IT, it is no different. Suppose you don't have a formal governance process, strategic planning meetings, strategy office, or other such formal mechanisms to help align the organization. In that case, you most likely still have a minor form of strategic planning in place, if nothing more than a goals and objectives method. If the entire organization is more of the status quo, unmeasured goals budget drives the initiatives type of organization—don't laugh, they exist in abundance—then you may want to somehow encourage an organized and formal strategic planning process throughout the organization. Suggest a performance or outcomes-based budgeting model, perhaps. If anything, as CIO, your IT Group can at least practice and demonstrate the formal, organized process, in conjunction with the method the rest of the organization uses as one way to help you sell the idea.

States of the IT Group

I mentioned the IT group's three states in chapter four,

regarding assessments and how vital it is to know which state your IT group was in for strategic planning efforts. The three distinct states of an IT group are broken into six areas that follow the core competencies. They are:

Level 1: Reactive state. We call this the *Smoke Jumper*, as coined by one of the managers I referred to earlier. I liked the term, so I kept it; it is very apropos.

Level 2: Proactive state. We call this the *Trusted Partner*. While it is a decent state to be in, it is not the best state to be in.

Level 3: Strategic enabler. We call this *innovating*.

As soon as you get to the strategic enabler state, you look around the first time and think, "there is nothing to fix!" Good! Now, get to innovating! The feeling of achieving that state is absolutely brilliant and, if you get there, then be proud. Especially if you didn't inherit it and had to work from smoke jumper to innovating over time like I did in Chattanooga.

The six areas we focus on when determining what state the IT group is in are projects, technology, processes, people, budget, and IT/organizational alignment. The core competencies cover all of the IT group's actual functions to deliver value and are what we measure; these six areas cover the competencies. Still, they are broader in scope, making it easier to assess the IT group's state.

REACTIVE STATE - SMOKE JUMPER

Level one is when the IT group is in a reactive state. By now, hopefully, you know this is not a state you want your IT group to be in. Let's look at each area. You are in a reactive state when:

PROJECTS
- Have no formal project management process;
- Projects are not governed, and most are focused on core IT delivery;
- Project benefits are unknown.

TECHNOLOGY
- The majority of IT systems are legacy or are in poor shape;
- Infrastructure is unstable;
- The application portfolio is unknown.

PROCESSES
- Processes are not performed well, consistent, or documented;
- Strategic and core processes are not known;
- Cost and performance of processes are not tracked or reviewed.

PEOPLE
- IT capabilities are unknown;
- IT organization design has not been planned;

- There is no clear career path for staff.

BUDGET
- IT spending is not tracked or is poorly tracked;
- Resource spending is unknown;
- Budget planning is ad hoc.

IT/ORGANIZATION ALIGNMENT
- The organization sees limited value in IT;
- No established IT governance;
- IT is federated.

Looking at the reactive state, you can see the many reasons why it's not very effective. No formal project management practices, procedures, or training means isolated—and perhaps not even funded—projects with a good chance of failure. Most of the projects in a reactive state have no real value to the organization or, at most, minimal value at a high cost. Why? Because there is no governance. A project portfolio in any organization should be analyzed and measured for performance. And, before any project begins, it needs to demonstrate a significant value to the organization. This is what cost-benefit analyses are for, why we track the outcomes, and how they ultimately impact the organization. This is why we figure out the break-even point (i.e. the point at which we have recovered the initial investment into the project). And why we create business cases complete with financial benefits of the outcomes, total return on the investment

(ROI) before deciding to invest in the project, and so on.

Then we move on to technology. If a majority of your IT systems are legacy systems, not updated or well maintained. Infrastructure is unstable. Or, perhaps you have one or more single points of failure. Your application portfolio is basically nonexistent. And you have no clue what's out there, let alone why it is out there. All this adds up to you not only being unable to innovate but at serious risk for ransomware attacks. Hello Atlanta, GA, Baltimore, MD, Knoxville, TN, St. Lucie, FL, Greenville, NC, New Orleans, LA, New Bedford, MA, Pensacola, FL, and Wilmer, TX, to name a few. There are quite a few cities, counties, and states out there that are still at risk and are just lucky at this point.

In a reactive state, processes are pretty much ad hoc and, at the very least, not documented, especially strategic processes, if those are even identified and known to begin with. Having your core and strategic processes listed is essential for continuing operations, disaster recovery, and even onboarding new IT staff.

This is a good segway into people. If it is one thing I am well known for, it is working for my staff. In a reactive state, your IT group's capabilities are unknown and not tracked. The IT group's organization design isn't strategically thought, out, but rather, just thrown together based on… yeah, nothing.

An example is, vacancies filled with warm bodies and looked at as capacity relies on the number of staff vs. capabilities department-wide. A.k.a., I need more people and 100 people is better than 75 talented and dedicated [A] people. If you hire the right people and pay them well, you can do a lot more, with a lot less. This leads to another issue in the reactive state IT group, or even the entire organization: no clear career path. I find this to be true of most public sector organizations, unfortunately. You typically only see it defined in the military or with police and fire departments as discussed in chapter three.

From a budget standpoint, IT spending is not tracked or is poorly tracked. Resources spending isn't known or not accounted for well. And budget planning is ad hoc at best. You can tell this quickly if the CIO sits down to do the budget and just asks people what they need in each IT group area, or worse, across the organization. That's ad hoc and not well planned. Looking at IT/ organization alignment from the reactive state viewpoint, we will see that the organization sees limited, if any, value in the IT group or tech itself. There is no established IT governance. Typically, you will see a federated IT model where every department— worst-case—or some areas of the organization all have their own IT groups, internal and specific to their area of expertise. Let me go on record right here and now; this is the worst possible way to run IT in any organization. I've mentioned this before. However, I think it needs repeating. Centralize your IT group first and foremost. It is not an easy thing to do, I know, I've had to do it. I'll share my experience doing this another time. For now, know it causes nothing but problems across the organization. Siloed communications and technology are pure evil.

Proactive State - Trusted Partner

Level two is a much better state, but not the best. If you are in this state, you are well on your way. This state we call the trusted partner. And here are the things to look for in each of the six areas:

Projects
- The organization is involved in project approval;
- IT balances strategic and operational projects;
- Project demand is known.

Technology
- A technology roadmap is defined;
- Operational costs are being reduced, and duplicate systems are decommissioned;
- Applications and infrastructure are enabling organization services.

Processes
- Core IT processes are performed and predictable;
- Strategic processes are being established;
- IT is automating business processes.
- People
- IT group is aligned by IT function;
- IT capabilities are known and established;
- Career planning is implemented and repeatable.

PEOPLE

- IT group is aligned by IT function;
- IT capabilities are known and established;
- Career planning is implemented and repeatable.

BUDGET

- IT is able to track project spending by multiple dimensions: costs, services, business lines, strategic goals, planning, etc.;
- Resource spending is predictable and reconciled;
- Costs of IT services are known.
- IT/Organization Alignment
- The organization is involved in setting IT direction;
- IT is centralized;
- IT is viewed as an enabler of business programs;
- IT governance is established and repeatable.

IT/ORGANIZATION ALIGNMENT

- The organization is involved in setting IT direction;
- IT is centralized;
- IT is viewed as an enabler of business programs;
- IT governance is established and repeatable.

Right away, you can see a significant difference between a reactive state and a proactive state. IT includes the rest of the organization in project planning and approval. The portfolio is balanced and well tracked. And the demand is known, as well as, the capacity for project completion. In the technology area, the IT group has a roadmap as part of the strategic plan. The IT group should be constantly looking for savings in all operational areas, by reducing any redundancy in systems. Systems that aren't needed or are not utilized, among other things. Applications and infrastructure are enabling the business processes and services provided by the rest of the organization. And, automation of business processes begins to show savings in time, effort, and money.

The IT group at this stage should be aligned by IT functions, such as having an IT project management office (PMO) operations section, infrastructure section, applications section, and service desk, within the IT group. All of the IT group's capabilities are well known and established. And, there is at least some simple form of career planning for IT staff. This one, as we know, is one of the more difficult areas to tackle in the public sector.

As for the budget and alignment with the rest of the organization, the IT group is remarkably better by getting the other parts of the organization involved in setting the IT group's direction. This is tough for many CIOs, and other public sector department heads, because they don't like other organization areas telling them how to run their department. Again, that is not what it's about and, please let that idea go. It's about planning the strategic direction of technology in the organization. If you don't collaborate with other areas—as I said in chapter five, build partnerships—you will be doomed to a continuously reactive state.

STRATEGIC ENABLER - INNOVATING

Level three is the crème de la crème of the three IT states. Not many IT groups make it all the way here. They may have some areas in the strategic enabler state, but the majority is usually proactive. Sometimes, this isn't the IT group's fault or the CIO's, but a product of the entire organization's leadership or current state. The genuinely great CIOs don't stop at IT. They partner with others in the organization to positively influence leadership in the right direction as best they can, which makes achieving the strategic enabler state for the IT group a little easier.

PROJECTS
- IT leads technology project recommendations for the organization;
- IT works with the organization to generate new sources of value and even revenue.

TECHNOLOGY
- IT uses/develops industry-leading technology;
- Disruptive technology enables the organization;
- Cloud technology is utilized, and a cloud-first approach could be taken.

Processes
- Processes are leading practices;
- IT is a master of business process reengineering and automation;
- Processes are optimized for cost reduction.

People
- IT group is aligned by services;
- Capabilities are leading practice;
- IT is best-of-breed at retaining and attracting talent.

Budget
- IT offers services at or below market rates;
- Budget is linked to value creation activities (outcomes);
- Strategic planning is the driving force in budget creation.

IT/Alignment Alignment
- IT supports and enables business innovation, industry awareness, and solution creation pathways.

In this wonderful state, IT leads project recommendations, instead of just taking orders for tech, and continuously works with the organization to generate new sources of value. The IT group develops industry-leading technology, especially in the smart cities era. Leading disruptive technology enables the organization and adds tremendous value to citizens in the community. Also, cloud technology is utilized a great deal more than in a proactive state. Any CIO who snubs their nose up at cloud computing doesn't really see the value or understand why it's the future, until the next significant disruption comes along, at least. Remember, great CIOs are visionaries and strategic enablers! This delightful state also means your processes are leading practices in the industry. You should experiment with different techniques and methods throughout your IT group, especially in agile. The IT group also becomes the master of business process reengineering and automation. It's great when the chief executive asks the IT group to help fix processes across the organization in conjunction with your partners because they trust and know the IT group can deliver.

The innovation state also means staff in the IT group are happier, more motivated, and far more productive. You align by service instead of function and see where more value is. The IT group has leading capabilities. And, you can hire and retain the best of the best in talent, if your pay scales allow for it, that is. For the strategic enabling CIO, the IT budget is connected to outcomes and value creation. The strategic plan is the driving force in budget preparation. This CIO also focuses on IT and organization alignment, ensuring IT supports business and technology innovation across the organization, creating industry awareness and solution creation paths.

Aligning IT with the Organization

You have heard the phrase a thousand times, or more: alignment with the organization—align this, align that, all on the same page, etc. Chapter six discussed the need to partner with the other departments in your organization, define and explain IT, and IT's purpose. Here is where we describe how IT adds value by aligning IT's mission and vision with the organization. First, let's look at the core elements you need to formulate your strategy for guiding IT in your organization. Remember, the primary theme should be adding value to the organization and the services the organization provides its customers (e.g. citizens/businesses, in the case of the public sector). We will look at these elements from what is called the strategic altitude scale. See figure 8-1.

Looking at the elements at their respective altitude gives you a good idea of their purpose and how they make up the big picture—synthesis. At 30,000 feet, the mission statement sets the overall purpose for your IT Group's existence. Below is your vision, without which you can have no effective strategy and have no direction. In the middle, you find the three portions that make up the primary difference between traditional budget-based goal/ objective planning and the balanced scorecard method (i.e. the four perspectives of your scorecard: strategic themes, objectives, and strategy map). At the 5,000 foot level, you find the performance measures and targets. Finally, you get down to ground level and into the trenches with the project and operational work needed

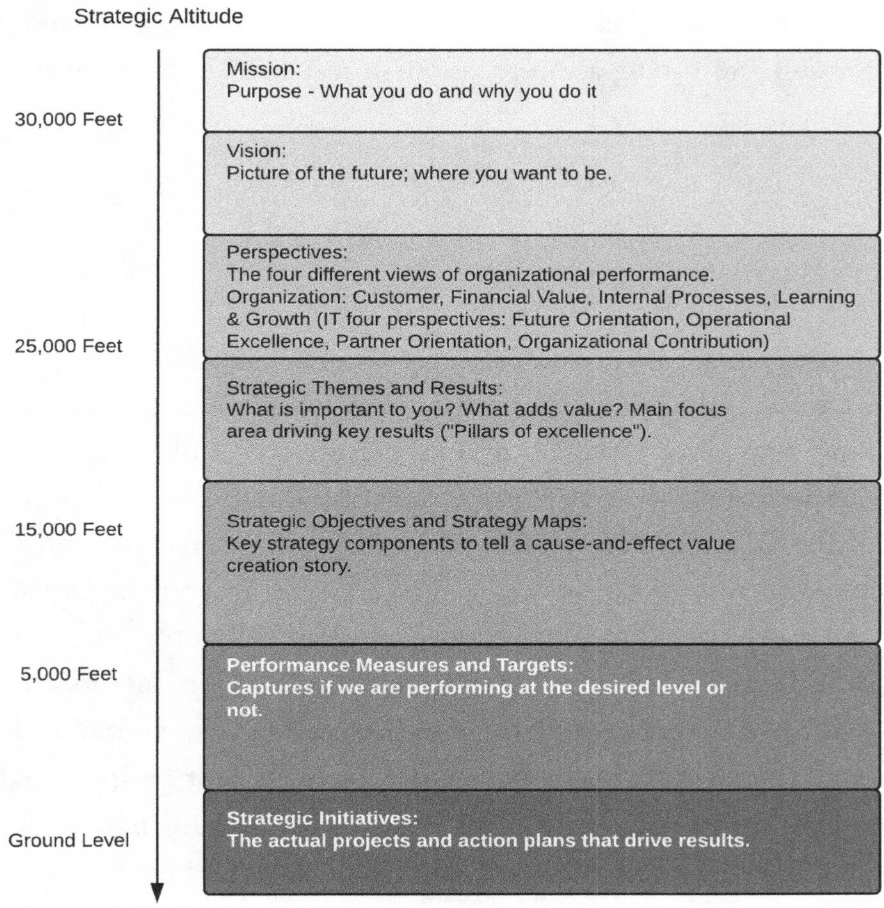

Strategic Altitude

30,000 Feet	Mission: Purpose - What you do and why you do it
	Vision: Picture of the future; where you want to be.
25,000 Feet	Perspectives: The four different views of organizational performance. Organization: Customer, Financial Value, Internal Processes, Learning & Growth (IT four perspectives: Future Orientation, Operational Excellence, Partner Orientation, Organizational Contribution)
	Strategic Themes and Results: What is important to you? What adds value? Main focus area driving key results ("Pillars of excellence").
15,000 Feet	Strategic Objectives and Strategy Maps: Key strategy components to tell a cause-and-effect value creation story.
5,000 Feet	Performance Measures and Targets: Captures if we are performing at the desired level or not.
Ground Level	Strategic Initiatives: The actual projects and action plans that drive results.

Figure 8-1: Strategic Altitude Scale

to fulfill the mission and vision. It all begins with setting your mission and having a future vision, as discussed in the previous chapter.

GAINING PERSPECTIVE

Referring back to the strategic altitude diagram, once you have established your IT group's mission and vision, you must now demonstrate the IT group's perspective. I like the term perspective not only as a way to describe a particular viewpoint of the IT group's performance but also to describe taking a flat two-dimensional object (e.g. your IT Group in abstract terms) and giving it a three-dimensional perspective. Simply put, you provide depth and meaning to what your IT group does to add value to the organization. The four perspectives of organizational performance refer to the Balanced Scorecard's four perspectives, established by Robert S. Kaplan and David P. Norton, in the early '90s. The Balanced Scorecard effectively changed how business performance is measured in the private sector, and has started to catch on in the public sector. The Balanced Scorecard is by no means a perfect management tool to measure performance, but it does an excellent job if used properly to get you in the right direction.

So, what are the four different perspectives of organizational performance? The original four perspectives were: Customer,

Financial Value, Internal Processes, and Learning & Growth. For public sector IT, I use a slightly different approach I call the Government IT Balanced Scorecard, a variation of the original. The Government IT Balanced Scorecard's four perspectives are Future Orientation, Partner & Citizen Orientation, Internal Perspective, and Organizational Contribution. Being the stickler for detail that I am, I adjusted one perspective slightly for my model related to the public sector by changing Customer Orientation to Partner & Citizen Orientation. However, for the most part, the measures are similar. Of course, you can modify the perspectives as you see best fit for your organization and mission. For an example of the Government IT Balanced Scorecard, see Figure 8-2:

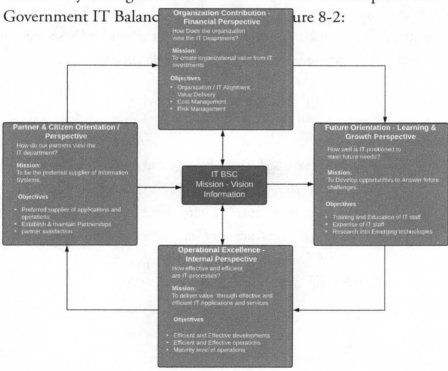

Figure 8-2: IT Balanced Scorecard

STRATEGIC THEMES

The strategic themes are the so-called "pillars of excellence." These themes define what is essential to your IT group, concerning the vision of the City. They basically help you define areas of concentration to align your overall strategy. For example, the strategic themes I use as a CIO are Operational Excellence, Standardization & Reuse, Technological Maturity, and Sustainability, what I believe are the four core themes to most any IT group. These strategic themes come into play in two ways during your strategic planning process. The first is to write statements—a paragraph or two—to define how each theme is important to your IT group and the organization. These are the statements I wrote for each of our strategic themes.

OPERATIONAL EXCELLENCE

The Department of Information Technology (DIT) will strive to be the most efficient and effective we can possibly be. We must constantly look to improve in every way possible and become as lean as possible. IT must have strong leadership and build a great culture and an attractive environment for the best IT talent. Then hire, develop, and retain solid performing IT staff.

STANDARDIZATION & REUSE

DIT will implement tailored industry standards and best practices throughout the department. IT will remain centralized, including the central acquisition of standardized technology purchasing and governance.

TECHNOLOGICAL MATURITY

DIT will plan and maintain our enterprise architecture appropriately using the correct methodology, tools, and the City's information capital. A core goal shall always be to keep the technology architecture up to date, and core systems interoperable, wherever feasible and possible, and focus on innovation.

SUSTAINABILITY

DIT will look to implement sustainable technologies whenever feasible. DIT will strive to utilize lean management practices and constantly improve our processes for peak efficiency. IT will also strive to provide a consistent and continuously improving user experience, focusing on formal IT governance, providing excellent core systems and processes, and being the provider of choice to our partners.

STRATEGY MAP

The second way the themes are used in the strategic planning process is to create your strategy map. This is essentially a visual representation of your core strategy and specific tactics (actions), tell a cause-and-effect value creation story.

As an example, figure 8-3 shows the strategy map for the City of Chattanooga's IT strategy:

It's easy to view the strategy map and get an excellent visual representation of value creation. For example, to achieve and maintain operational excellence, IT needs strong leadership, via a CIO, DCIO, Directors, Managers, Supervisors, and Staff, building a great open communication culture. This environment will attract talent easier, making for more substantial teams, which is a crucial component of sustainable practices (see chapter two: Building a Great Culture). You can start to see each bubble's cause and effect relationship, (follow the arrows up through each perspective on the left side of the map), and how each theme, (the pillars along the bottom of the map), plays a part in value creation. Feel free to use this exact example as is or as a template to create your own strategy map.

STRATEGIC PLANNING ENGINE

By now, I think you have figured out I love using famous quotes to drive home message themes, so why not here too. To

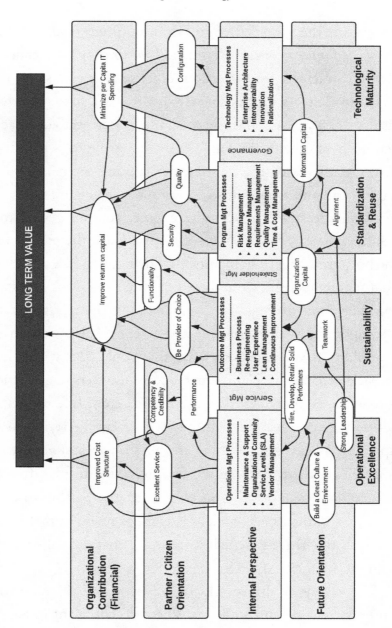

Figure 8-3: Strategy Map

quote from the Art of War, Sun Tsu said, "*Strategy without tactics is the slowest route to victory. Tactics without strategy is the noise before defeat.*" Strategy is your method to get to a specific set of results. It's your plan. As previously stated, you can't strategize without vision. Then you use strategic goals and objectives to drive actions, actions being the tactics Sun Tsu was referring to, which in turn drives results. I call this the strategic planning engine, because I'm a gear head and a car nut, so it's apropos. See Figure 8-4.

With the strategic planning engine, you are geared toward results and driven by vision—see what I did there? The line at the bottom is wiggly, going up and down much like a stock price. That represents reality, numbered in years. You don't just start off to achieve something; and, bam, you are magically there and in a straight line with no outside interference. If life were that way, I wouldn't have needed to write this book. You will fail, have setbacks, changes in plans, emergencies, disasters (e.g. hurricanes, tornadoes, earthquakes, terrorist attacks, etc.). Life happens and will continue to happen. Murphy will always be trying to screw up your strategy and planning efforts; so, you best get used to it. You will get there eventually if you look at your plan frequently and adjust it as needed. You will never just be able to create a strategy and then never look at it again or revise it; that is simply not realistic. There is actually a term for that; it's called strategic plan on the shelf (SPOTS).

The engine is driven and fueled by vision, looking to that future state you want to be at. Where do you want to be? What

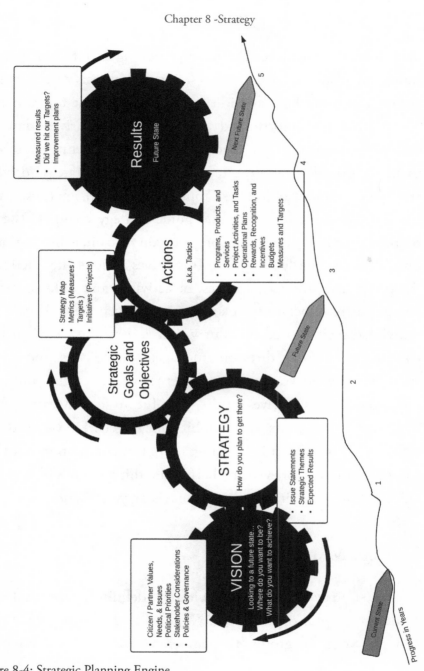

Figure 8-4: Strategic Planning Engine

do you want to achieve? I'm not just talking about your vision statement. You can have a vision for several aspects or one bold vision. You could have a vision for smart cities, one for your IT group processes, so forth, and so on. Each vision drives strategy, (i.e. how you plan to get there). Use issue statements, strategic themes, and discuss expected results early. Strategy drives strategic goals and objectives. Your strategy map, metrics, and measures show performance and guide strategy changes. These become your initiatives or the projects you take on, achieving the outcomes you are looking for. This drives actions (i.e. tactics): the programs, products, services, or activities and tasks to help you get there. Operational plans come into play here. These are individual plans, based on your vision and strategy, devised by your deputy CIO(s), directors, managers, supervisors, and even staff. This is where you set targets and measures to ensure you stay on target. And that drives results, your future state. Measure the outcomes, not outputs. Did you hit your targets? Do we need to refine our plan? When innovating, it's not uncommon to not hit a target right away or even at all. The vital thing to do is if you fail, fail fast, learn from it, and drive on revising your tactics.

ROAD MAPS

No strategy is complete without defining a technology roadmap for your organization. Notice, I said your organization and not your IT group. Remember, you are focused on the technology strategy for the organization, not just your IT group. Think of your road map as a plot in time. By 2024 you wish to have X in place. By 2025 you want X expanded to include Y, Z, and so on. You can do this for just about anything in the organization, including typical internal projects like infrastructure upgrades, if you really want. I typically just keep to innovative and transformational things/projects on my road map, if possible. But, I have included just about everything of value in past maps, especially when building an IT group up from a reactive state's ruins. In that case, you really have no choice, because innovating is impossible in that state. Thus you must build the foundation first.

Your road map should essentially only contain three types of things. Initiatives, capabilities, and strategies—including what are known as micro strategies. The map should display each of these items aligned in one of your four pillars of excellence: Sustainability, Operational Excellence, Technological Maturity, or Standardization and Reuse. Then select terms in years when you wish to complete these initiatives, have these capabilities, or enact that strategy. You can do this in any length of time, really. However, I tend to do three terms.

Short term: within the next two years.

Medium-term: within the next three to four years.

Long term: within the next five to six years.

Here are some examples from the first strategic plan I wrote for the City of Chattanooga in early 2014 for the 2014/2015 fiscal year. Under Operational Excellence, we had a few capabilities/initiatives. These were based on the gap analysis I did my first year with the City.

World-class service desk (Short Term: 2016-2017)

* Building and maintaining a world-class service desk to improve our customer service across the board and enhance our first-line service staff performance.

Resource capacity

* Continue building and developing our resources by establishing partnerships with vendors, sister agencies and promoting/recruiting top talent.

Overhead reduction and thinning (Ongoing)

* Continue to cut costs and reduce waste (Six-Sigma) for the highest possible performance.

Well defined service catalog

* To better establish the full capability of DIT and define what DIT can and can't do for City departments and agencies. Items outside our catalog may be vendor-driven.

These can be anything you need to work on or want to achieve by a specific date. Be careful what you put in here if you plan on making the strategic plan or the road map public. These days, I don't advise making written strategic plans public if they contain anything of critical nature to the organization, giving away a specific state you are in. This could be used to target vulnerable systems. If you want to publish something, make a separate document that only lists your road map and general strategy for smart cities initiatives or similar. But nothing that highlights any possible vulnerabilities you may have. Like your continuing operations/disaster recovery plans, keep your real strategy internal and eyes only to those who have operational awareness and security training. This includes vendors who have not signed a nondisclosure agreement or some other legal instrument your attorney's office has devised to protect you. In most states, sunshine laws do not apply to the documentation that could put the organization at risk.

CHAPTER NINE
MONITOR AND MEASURE

" However beautiful the strategy, you should occasionally look at the results." ~ Winston Churchill

So far, we have established that great CIOs are good leaders, strategic planners with a solid vision of IT's future state in the organization and can devise a clear strategy to achieve that vision. Also, they are constantly assessing their IT group's performance. You have a vision of where you want to be and set an overall technology strategy for your organization, so now what? We have to break that into actions (i.e. tactics), setting goals to measure our results—outcomes and their impact, not outputs. We don't measure inputs or outputs because that information is not valuable to us in the overall scheme of things. So how do we measure our outcomes? Where do we start? How do we know what goals to set to strategize the best way to achieve them? Where do the baseline measures come from?

All valid questions; and I know this can be very confusing. To explain this a succinctly as possible, let's review our gap analysis example for better service, usually referred to as customer service. Remember from chapter four, we had a performance gap we needed to fill going from our current state of service satisfaction of 70.23% to 85% or higher in just one year. That's our goal. If you did your assessment correctly and analyzed your gaps in performance for the area of concern, in this case, service satisfaction, you have essentially already set your goals. Do that for every gap analysis, and each one should have at least one goal or more. Where you get the baseline measures for those assessments is pretty easy too.

I once had a CIO tell me that you can't measure certain things; it is just not possible to measure everything. That is not true at all. Everything can be measured if you look at it correctly and know what you should and shouldn't be trying to measure in the first place. Knowing the difference between what data you can put together to make informed decisions, and what is data that adds no value to the decision making process, is an important skill to have as a CIO. Let's stick with our poor service gap example. What is useful to know about our service performance regarding our service desk? What does the service desk do? It provides tier one and sometimes tier two tech support and customer service. It also acts as the face of the IT group in most cases with general users in the organization. So how do you measure how well the service desk is performing? Most of us think of customer satisfaction ratings, right? Yes. How do you get an idea of your satisfaction if you haven't been tracking this? First, to get a baseline, you can send out an organization-wide survey asking questions like how satisfied are you overall with <IT group's name> service performance? Or something more complex like a matrix question asking the same problem but with different answers. Like, how satisfied are you that your IT group keeps the systems up and running? How satisfied are you that your IT group delivers promised services on a timely basis? How satisfied are you that your IT group helps you use technology effectively? And so on.

Generally speaking, a simple one-question overall satisfaction rating will get you going in the right direction, providing you with a good baseline of what you are dealing with. Later, I suggest moving to a robust service desk platform, like Atlassian Service Desk for Jira—Atlassian did not pay me to say that I just love Atlassian products and highly recommend them. There are many others out there; and they all do similar things. The point is you want an easy way to track service requests and user satisfaction with those requests and set and measure service level agreements in a consistent manner. For our example, let's assume we sent out a survey and already. The results of the survey have given us our baseline metric to start. Over time, as we make changes, we remeasure performance with another survey, or with our data from our service desk software to determine our progress. If progress is good, we're doing something correctly. If it's not, then time to go back to the drawing board and find a better way. Also, be sure not to get caught in the insanity loop of trying the same thing, over and over, hoping for a different result each time. Get to the root cause of your performance problems (i.e. by performing a root cause analysis).

GOALS NOT SO CLEAR

When teaching a seminar on goal making and strategic planning, I always hear concerns about creating goals. "Goals for X department isn't as easy and straightforward as with you IT guys." Not true. Let me show you how. This is similar to people thinking that outputs and outcomes are the same things; they are not. Measuring the outcome enables you to know if you have achieved the goal. Here's one example when speaking to the fire department chief during the seminar: I ask, what are some of your current goals and measurements? The fire chief stated, "One goal we have is we want to educate more people about smoke alarm safety and the importance of checking them and changing batteries regularly, and we measure how many times we hold free classes for the community." I told him that wasn't a goal. Again I get the same response. "It's hard to measure what we do and subsequently hard to set goals." I put it to him this way. "Why?" "Why, what?" he said. "Why do you want to educate people about smoke alarm maintenance and safety?" He thought about it a second and said, "well, to make them aware of the dangers of not having a working smoke alarm in the house." Again I asked, why? He stared at me quizzically. I said, "Why do you want to make them aware of those dangers?" He said, "to keep them safe." I said, "A-ha! So you want to protect them?" "Yes!" he said. "Exactly what we want to do." I then said, "then now you have your goal. Your goal is to reduce the number of lives lost due to faulty or no smoke alarms in homes." His eyes lit up, I knew it had just clicked. Keep asking why. Why do you want to pave the roads? To reduce damage to vehicles. Why do you want to put reflectors on the street, stop signs at an intersection, or increase communications, or… It's all the same. Just ask why you want to do something, what is the ultimate objective you are looking to achieve. That's your goal. Increasing communications, painting lines on a road, teaching smoke alarm classes are all actions-processes. The number of classes you teach could be one metric to measure. Then compare that to the number of injuries or fatalities due to fires where no spoke alarm was present or functioning properly. Then you can see if those classes are doing any good for the community.

I used non-IT related items in these examples to demonstrate that the method of setting goals is the same regardless of the area of the organization you are monitoring. What's important, is you are measuring the correct data and you know what those measurements tell you, in order to make the best decisions. More on IT measures later.

Inputs vs. Outputs vs. Outcomes

In general, inputs drive processes (i.e. activities), which drive outputs, which feedback from those outputs drives more inputs. This is an iterative process in project management, and the end result is the outcome (i.e. the part we measure). Essentially we are measuring the impact the outcome has on the organization. Again, we don't measure inputs or outputs; we measure outcomes and their impact. And goal measurements should always have one of these three words: reduce, increase, or maintain.

Using the smoke alarm example I mentioned, the input is the goal: reduce the number of lives lost due to faulty or no smoke alarms in homes. Processes would be, develop more courses and course materials, distribute free smoke alarms, etc. The output would be, more people educated in the community or people in need get free smoke alarms. The outcome is more smoke alarms in homes, thus reduced loss of life. The impact is a stronger, safer community and lives saved. Looking at IT and our service example, again, the input is our goal: to increase our satisfaction rating from 70.23% to 85% or higher by a specific date. That's another thing to remember; always set a time frame to achieve the goal. Processes can increase IT operations skillsets, cross-training, enhance incident response, request communication, reporting ability, etc. Outputs would be service desk techs better educated and capable. The outcome would be satisfaction ratings go up. And the impact is IT is more respected, more trusted, gets a better reputation and ultimately, what? I'm always listening for Robb to scream it out…, Adding more actual value to the organization!

Can we set and measure process and activity goals? Of course.

Remember, anything can be measured. But, don't spend your time measuring things so much that you inhibit progress towards the goals as a result.

KEY PERFORMANCE INDICATORS

There is a whole slew of KPIs you can measure in IT; just refer back to chapter four and the list of competencies. I do try to measure all that is relevant to our IT group and our operations. Here are just a few examples:

Change Management KPIs
1. Percentage reduction in unauthorized changes;
2. Percentage reduction in the average time to make changes;
3. Percentage reduction/or maintained in unsuccessful changes;

Security KPIs
4. The average time elapsed between vulnerability or weakness discovery and the implementation of corrective action;
5. Percentage increase of email phishing attempts that are reported by users and not clicked through.

Availability KPIs
6. Percentage reduction in the unavailability of services;
7. Percentage improvement in the meantime between failures (MTBF);

8. Percentage reduction in the meantime to repair/recover (MTTR).

Capacity KPIs

9. Reduction in the overcapacity of the IT group;
10. Reduction in business interruption caused by the lack of IT capacity.

Service Desk KPIs

11. Percentage decrease in length of service desk request queues;
12. Percentage increase in met SLAs.

Release KPIs

13. Percentage reduction in build failures;
14. Percentage reduction in the number of urgent releases.

These are just 14 examples, however, there are over 200 plus KPI's you could measure for IT. Do you need to measure them all? No, not always. It's nice to have that information eventually as long as you can automate the measurement and get a dashboard for it. However, at first focus on what really matters and what you are trying to assess or fix. These are only a sample of what can and should be measured in your IT group. For a complete list, visit the companion website for this book.

DATA DRIVEN DECISIONS

I can't stress enough how critical data are to digital

transformation and innovation. Collecting data from across the organization allows you the ability to mine that data for trends, especially if you can build a data warehouse and automatically feed it. Look for anomalies you might not otherwise see, and correlate one departments' functions to how it impacts other areas of the organization. This means that every decision made by you or anyone else using the data to make decisions is based on fact and not speculation. It's not just about collecting data and measuring performance. You should build a data-driven culture, too. You can do this exclusively in your IT group; but, your entire organization should also be data driven to make good decisions, make progress, save money, and innovate! As the CIO, you and your IT group are there to help and do what? Yup, provide value.

PART THREE
THE BUSINESS OF GOVERNMENT

CHAPTER TEN
AGILE AND INNOVATIVE

❝*Sometimes when you innovate, you make mistakes. It is best to admit them quickly, and get on with improving your other innovations."* ~ *Steve Jobs.*

Let's look at the crème de la crème of government today, innovation. I know, I know, "Hey Brent, isn't that an oxymoron: government and innovation?" At one point, I suppose it was and still today, in some government agencies, yeah. But, if that's the case where you are, you can help bring change.

So, how exactly does one go about innovating in government? Well, there is a reason the innovation chapter comes towards the end of the book. You must have every other concept in this book covered, from end to end. You must be a good leader and have good leaders in your staff. You must build a great culture. You must be well organized and have some semblance of IT governance. You must develop great relationships with your partners across the organization. You must have a vision and plan well. You must measure and monitor your performance, while constantly looking to improve yourself, your staff, and your IT group as a whole. All of these things are absolutely essential to innovation anywhere, much less the public sector. Also, the IT group also must be at the very minimum in a primarily strategic enabler state. The only way you could innovate in a proactive state is by ignoring many things you don't want to ignore. And you can not innovate in a stifled reactive environment; it just isn't possible. Does your IT group need to be perfect? Of course not, nor will it ever be, but you can always strive for perfection knowing you can't ever get there. You will improve over time.

Failure is an Option

"It's fine to celebrate success, but it is more important to heed the lessons of failure." - Bill Gates.

Any CIO worth their salt knows to err is human. They make mistakes and learn more from those mistakes than any successes. These CIOs also know the old adage of "nothing ventured, nothing gained." If you want to innovate, you have to adopt a mentality that failure happens; and, it is an option. If you build and encourage the IT group culture, correctly, you will have diligent and precise staff, in their planning, research, and development. They minimize risks. And, as a result, the failures come quickly and are not all that bad. Just remember to fail fast;

learn from the failure; and move on quickly to succeed.

These innovative CIOs set up research and development programs and encourage ideas from anywhere in the organization, not just their managerial or leadership staff. Your staff shouldn't go off half-cocked and unprepared either. Don't confuse being innovative to mean doing anything you want, without planning for it or doing things half-assed. If a mistake is made or an experiment or actual project fails, it's usually due to some unforeseen thing the planning didn't pick up. This is where Agile methods tend to prevail in IT. Perform a root-cause analysis, as appropriate. Figure out the problem and correct it. Learn from the experience. Then, try again or move on to the next innovation. And, having an environment where a failure is an option isn't just a concept I am suggesting out of the blue; it is part of the continuous improvement and innovation processes, used the world over by leaders in countless organizations, most famously by the Toyota Motor Corporation. It is not uncommon to find failed projects leading to significant changes, which eventually lead to super successes. Like with the executives of the worldwide group of Toyota companies, great CIOs know they don't always have the answers; and they or their staff can't always get it right the first time. That is okay. Failure is an option.

The argument I hear a lot regarding failure being an option in the public sector is, "you are wasting taxpayers' dollars if you fail." My answer to that is technically, you end up wasting more money in the long run by implementing inferior products, not innovating, and just watching the bottom line, rather than absorbing a few low-cost failures along the way (i.e. the cost of doing business). But, that is also why we employ agile methods. The easiest and correct way to fail fast in public sector IT is through agile approaches. You are able to change directions quickly and adapt to the situation, far faster than with traditional waterfall methods, or worse, no methods at all. Agile methods help minimize the cost of doing business. The small failures, or setbacks, along the way allow you to innovate faster. Thus you succeed faster. And, even though you may have had a few failures along the way, you are still saving money in the long run.

AGILE AND PROJECT MANAGEMENT

I've mentioned agile quite a bit in this chapter and several others as well. So, for those of you who don't know what agile is, allow me to elaborate. While there are agile methods, like DevOps, which do not necessarily look at a better way to perform project management—more so than a better method to run an entire IT group—there are also agile project management methods. Let's start with an agile project management perspective, since it is the most prevalent and well-defined of the agile methodologies. However, first, let us look back at traditional project management practices. In the general sense, project management typically calls upon the waterfall method for most predictable projects. The waterfall method is great for building houses, skyscrapers, or filming movies because in all of those outcomes (i.e the end result of a project), the processes are relatively the same and predictable. For example, you must first build the foundation of a house before you can create the walls, which in turn must be completed before you put the roof on. This method is not good at all for most IT projects, specifically software engineering/development projects. However, the waterfall method will work well for deploying new PCs in a department or across an organization, because there isn't much variation in such a project. Again, it's predictable. You select the hardware, plan the rollout, and go. I know I'm simplifying things. And, there is much more to a technology deployment than that. However, it serves the purpose of demonstrating not much changes from start to finish. One hardware rollout is the same, if not at least very similar, to another rollout three years later. There is very little, if any variation, that requires going back to the drawing board, so to speak. For other IT projects that are specifically variable in nature, such as with software development primarily, the waterfall method doesn't work well. Take a look at the diagram of the waterfall method in figure 10-1 to see what I mean.

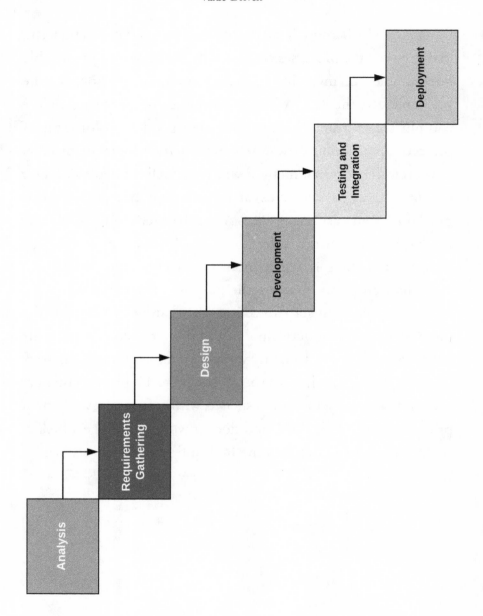

Figure 10-1: Waterfall Diagram

Let's run through a software engineering project, using the waterfall method. We start with an analysis where the purpose of the application is determined. Then, we gather requirements. Requirements gathering is a crucial stage in the waterfall method. If the requirements aren't gathered correctly, the whole project could be in jeopardy, wasting a lot of time and money, as a result. Yet, here's the rub; no matter how well you think you have gathered the requirements, what you develop will not meet the stakeholder's expectations a majority of the time. Once done with requirements gathering, we next move into design, where the application interface is designed, as well as all the other components like databases, functions, etc.—no need to get into the details here. Then comes development, which is where the actual coding comes into play. A waterfall-based software engineering project is usually the longest part of the project, as well as, the most critical and costly to repeat or change. Then, we move on to testing and integration (i.e. where the alpha and beta testing are usually performed). Software is integrated into the appropriate systems. Then, finally, the deployment phase, where the software is released.

Suppose you have made it this far without any changes. Great, however, chances are when the final product is seen and tested by the stakeholder I bet they aren't entirely happy with the outcome; or perhaps they are at first glance. Still, once they start using it for a few months, they may begin to see things that should be changed, and not what the stakeholders originally expected. Or, they claim that it is not what they asked for, even if you have a signed requirements document showing precisely the requirements you built into the system. This is because it's not as easy for most people to visualize exactly what they want, or more importantly, what they need.

Now let us imagine that you get past the first few stages of the project and get into the system or software development. Suddenly, there is a requirements change (i.e. change order), one that changes code that has already been written, tested, and fully integrated into the system—based on the first set of requirements. However, now that those requirements have changed, even just the slightest amount, it means the engineers are forced to start over. Now they must gather the new requirements, design around them, and then continue, by rewriting a lot of code to meet the changed requirements. When it comes to software engineering, this is a significant downfall of the waterfall method. You just went from development all the way back to requirements gathering with a single change to requirements, which means you must redesign, then redevelop, etc. You can see how that is a complete waste of time and, subsequently, money, especially if this cycle continues several times before you finally get close to what the stakeholders actually want.

There is a whole other conversation we could have about managing stakeholders and their expectations, likely turning into an entire book by itself; so I won't get into that here.

Waterfall problems really kill the morale of the development team working on the project, who now have to start all over again because they developed a product based on a specific set of requirements that have now changed. This tends to push deadlines out and put projects over budget, too. Agile helps prevent these things. See figure 10-2.

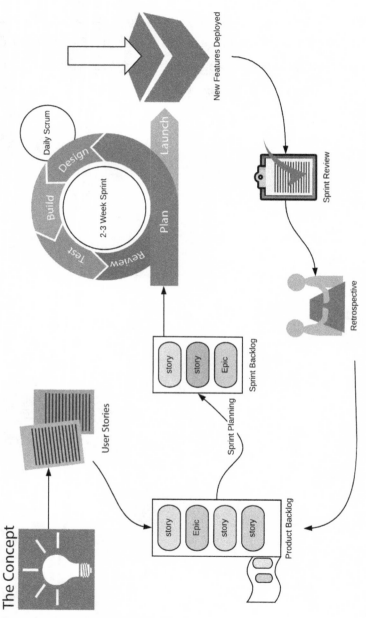

Figure 10-2: Agile Method Diagram

The Agile Software Development Life Cycle (SDLC) is an iterative approach, performed in sprints. The entire life cycle is completed in each sprint. The Sprint is planned. The first iteration is designed, then coded, tested, and reviewed. At the end of each sprint, you have a fully functioning, technically deployable, slice of the final product. That is an overly simplified description of the agile SDLC sprint process itself. And, I'm only going to touch on the high level overview of the Scrum method for development, because you could write an entire book on agile methodologies alone, which many have.

The sprint is only a part of the scrum process. Requirements are gathered into a backlog for the product owner to then sort by priority. The product owner is basically the primary stakeholder, with the most knowledge about how the system will be used and why. The most critical features or requirements are filtered to the top by the product owner. The sprint team could consist of developers, UX designers, database specialists, and testers. The first meeting between the sprint team and the product owner, after requirements gathering, is known as a backlog refinement meeting. During this time, the product owner(s) will refine the backlog and put the most important user stories at the top of the backlog. From there, the sprint team will have a separate sprint planning meeting where they decide the total value of the user stories—which later determines the amount of work the team can take on during a single sprint. This is called velocity. The team will then break the user stories into tasks needed to complete the functionality of the story. Then they will decide who will handle which tasks during the sprint. All of this information is kept on a Kanban Board, and as tasks and user stories are completed, they are moved across the board to the proper next stage.

Every day during the sprint, the team members get together with the Scrum Master discussing a few things in what is called the daily scrum (i.e. a 15-minute maximum standup meeting). Each team member answers three questions:

1. What did you accomplish yesterday?
2. What are you working on today?
3. Are there any impediments in your way?

The questions are designed to ensure everyone is on the same page with how the work is progressing. At the end of the sprint, the team has a full-functioning slice of the final product. Every feature in the stories chosen for the sprint is complete. And, during the sprint review meeting, the product owner tests them, or is given a demonstration, then marks the user stories from the sprint complete. If one is not done, it goes back into the backlog for the next sprint. An important concept here is the predetermined definition of the term completed, as agreed upon by the team and the product owner, early on in the project. From here, the team has a retrospective on the sprint. What worked? What could change? Then, back to the product backlog to start on planning the next sprint.

Again, this is a significantly simplified explanation, but should give you a basic understanding of the scrum process to get you started exploring the concepts.

Now, a quick note on the Scrum Master position. This is not a management position and does not supervise the development team. The purpose of the Scrum Master is to help facilitate the team, keep the meetings and documentation on track, and help remove impediments to the team, and keep the team moving forward. Also, the Scrum Master acts as a shield to keep product owners, department managers, project managers, and other people from disturbing the team during the sprints. It plays a critical role in making agile work with Scrum. Chattanooga's Scrum Masters are full time roles, housed in the IT Project Management Office and assigned to work with various scrum teams. An important concept is the fact, the teams should be self-managing and self-organized. The Scrum Master does not make assignments. Instead, the team members decide what they will work on during the sprint, based on their area of expertise. It is a fantastic concept that works very well in most cases and can be applied to other areas of the IT group, or even the entire organization.

PEAK ACADEMY

In the last chapter, I touched on data and data-driven culture.

One of the things that sets Chattanooga apart from other municipalities when it comes to innovation and smart cities is the fact Chattanooga has a great data-driven culture, thanks to the fantastic Office of Performance Management and Open Data (OPMOD). My friend and colleague, Tim Moreland, the Director of OPMOD—I still just call him the Chief Data Officer—runs a fantastic program, called the Chattanooga Peak Academy. Based on the original Denver Peak Academy, it's very similar to other lean/six-sigma training, but geared specifically for government agencies. This isn't just a process improvement class for department administrators or other leaders in the city.

Peak is for any employee, from anywhere across the city, specifically those on the front lines doing the work and living the business processes every day. In simplest terms it is a program that empowers employees to look for waste. Specifically, the eight wastes of six-sigma. Staff find processes around the city they have control over and evaluate, fix, or change those processes to be more efficient (i.e. Lean).

The Chattanooga Peak Academy is designed to take the best processes and methods from lean six-sigma, process improvement, human centered design change management, and behavior nudging from the private sector, teaching those methods to the employees doing the work on the front lines of city departments. It is often these very same employees who will be asked to implement a top down innovation mandate or improvement program. As a result, when you empower them directly, they buy into the change quickly, since it is coming from them, instead of from the top down. This empowers all employees across the city to enact change and seek out issues in processes or systems that not only cause them headaches, but also cause citizens headaches. For this process to work well, city leadership and management needs to be on board, also enabling the right culture to allow these changes to happen. It is an evolving process that, so far is making Chattanooga a much smarter, citizen focused, and more efficient municipality.

INNOVATION DISTRICTS

Think about innovating and what it takes to do so. You can't really plan innovation like it's a project. Do you call people into a room and say, "Hey! Let's innovate! I want ideas on the table right now!" No, it doesn't always work that way. You can't just throw people in a room and say, "let's come up with great ideas that will change the way we currently do things." Innovation, in most cases, is spontaneous and happens on the fly. That's where an innovation district comes into play. Also, it's one reason the Chattanooga Department of IT had a work from anywhere policy in place since the creation of the innovation district.

Collisions or people and ideas, and by that I mean my staff running into people from other agencies, companies, areas of the city, etc. These people discussing things in a natural way, as we humans tend to do. That's where sparks of innovation happen best.

Where ideas are formed or reformed. That is the concept behind an innovation district in a municipality. It provides collaboration space (e.g. open work areas) where people from various areas and disciplines can mingle and discuss ideas, promoting the concept of people getting out of the office and mingling with other experts in a variety of fields and disciplines. These off the cuff discussions lead to more innovative ideas and drive the community forward.

SMART CITIES

I am not going to get into the weeds here. However, since we are on the topic of innovation, I want to very briefly touch on another buzzword, Smart City. To date, there is no formal definition of what a smart city really is. I mean, are cities really smart? Doesn't calling a city a smart city imply that a smart city was once a dumb city? Personally, I don't like the term smart city. Most of my colleagues across the nation agree; yet, alas the phrase was coined and has stuck ever since. The way I see it, cities never stop improving and are either growing or declining all the time. So, in reality, a city is never really complete, only geting smarter, or less so, over time and with changes in technology.

As far as the tech behind smart cities initiatives, there is some pretty cool stuff out there. One example is in Chattanooga, where we decided to put cameras with GPS and accelerometers in all our vehicles for tracking and safety. However, the cameras in the garbage/recycling trucks were chosen specifically because those are really the only vehicles in a municipality that travel on just about every road. That means we could then use the footage streamed from those cameras. Apply artificial intelligence and machine learning algorithms to the footage to identify pot-holes, blighted property, or even tell if someone didn't put their trash can out for pickup. People sometimes call and say that their garbage pickup was missed, even though the City managed to get the neighbors on either side of them. As repairs are made to roads, the system would track the repair in real time. We would have all sorts of data on how long repairs lasted. The City could combine that data with data from traffic cameras to see how traffic loads on that repair affected it over time, and so on. The possibilities for smart cities tech is practically endless in today's world of the Internet of Things (IoT).

Since cities, you, your IT group, and the organization itself are constantly in flux. It's up to you and your chief executives to lead the charge, push innovation, get your city, county, or state moving in the right direction and become more innovative, faster, and better!

CHAPTER ELEVEN
GOVERNMENT AS A BUSINESS

“We have the best government that money can buy.”
—Mark Twain

In this final chapter, I thought we should finish up all of this value creation with the examination of the business of government, rather, the business conducted by governments. It is possible to view governments, at least local and state governments, as a business. Some CIOs have an entrepreneurial mindset that favors running the IT group, or the government organization itself, similar to a business: efficient, lean, and performance-based, as previously discussed. But let's look a little deeper and see what can be done to go a little further with these concepts.

The idea of running government like a business is not a new concept. In fact, the idea has been around and even debated for years. Government and business comparisons going back as far as the history of public administration, itself. Running a government organization like a business has been called a mantra, associated closely with new public management (NPM) reform movements, steming from business-type approaches to government, and utilized during the Reagan and Thatcher administrations of the 1980s[1]. I think you have figured out by now, I have always favored using efficient business practices and modern management concepts over heavily bureaucratic methods. I sometimes refer to this concept as Government as a Business, GaaB for short— Yes, it's a play on the whatever as a service type acronyms like, Software as a Service, Infrastructure as a Service, etc. GaaB techniques basically encompass all the techniques in this book. It emphasizes being innovative; and, nothing drives innovation like competition.

Now, there are plenty opposed to looking at government being run specifically as a business, I have even had CIOs and chief executives laugh at the notion, describing me as radical. These naysayers provide all sorts of reasons why it can't be done. Mind you, not shouldn't be done, but can't be done, as though it is entirely impossible. There are two main opposition arguments I encounter most:

The first argument is that government organizations cannot be profitable. Governments don't have to compete to deliver services or business. Ergo, since a firm in the private sector has to compete and be profitable, a government cannot be run like a business. The profitability argument's logic is summarized as *"not everything that is profitable is of social value, and not everything of social value is profitable[2]."* In other words, it would be absurd to attempt sustaining a government service entirely on the premise that the service had to generate a profit to survive, even though the service provided does have a specific social value.

This argument regarding profitability is primarily sound. I don't dispute the fact government should not entirely be run by sustaining a total profit the same way a firm in the private sector would. Not to mention, governments have to run under a different set of rules. I say mostly sound, because a government can sell a product or service to generate revenue supplementing traditional revenue streams used for daily operations. I have encountered some government organizations that have discussed doing this during the 2008 recession, to help make ends meet. Usually, this involves their IT groups (e.g. selling a piece of software developed in-house or paid consulting for other organizations). I've even heard of some selling advertising space on their websites—don't do that, by the way.

The second argument is government organizations do not compete. As a result, the lack of competition is the primary reason services provided by local and state government agencies are obnoxiously unreliable and slow—"moving at the speed of government," or "good enough for government." The logic is government serves as the only entity able to offer those specific services—monopoly (e.g. vehicle registration, business licensing, courts, airports, and so on). Because there is no one else with whom to compete, the service levels fall to absurdly inadequate levels and remain in the customer service basement ad infinitum. Anyone who has ever stood in line at a North Carolina Department of Motor Vehicles office to get a license plate knows precisely what I'm talking about. However, saying government agencies do not have to compete like a business for customers, thus having no incentive to provide good customer service or be efficient and frugal, is a significantly flawed argument. Suppose a government organization is inefficient, highly bureaucratic, bloated, and the government employees even rude, lazy, or unprofessional. In that case, it is because they choose to be, not because they have to be. Not all government organizations are like that, in part or whole. Yet, unfortunately, the stigma is very real in the public's perception of government as lazy and ineffective. Regardless, the fact is, governments do compete.

KEEP MOVING ON

Henry Ford said, "*it is not the employer who pays the wages. Employers only handle the money. It is the customer who pays the wages.*" He was right on the money, literally. The reality is, local and state governments do, in a way, actually have competition. The customers they compete for are the citizens and businesses currently in their area, as well as, new citizens and businesses that may settle in their area and stay long-term. Thus, it brings revenue, jobs, a better quality of life, and even a better reputation. My fellow Major League Baseball fans know exactly what I'm talking about. Look at what happened in 1964 when the then Milwaukee Braves franchise decided to move to Atlanta. They had only been in Milwaukee for about 12 years, coming from Boston, where they were the Boston Braves. Think about why they left Boston in the first place. When they moved to Milwaukee in 1952, they brought with them a record 1,826,297 National League fans to Milwaukee[3]. That's a significant boost to the local economy.

Unfortunately for Milwaukee at the time, that boost then left twelve years later for a better deal in Atlanta, where the Braves have been ever since. The same thing happens with other major sports teams and businesses of all types. For example, the Houston Oilers who moved to Nashville, Tennessee and became the Tennessee Titans, and the Brooklyn Dodgers who moved to Los Angeles, California to become the L.A. Dodgers, and many others. And, it was not just sports franchises or businesses. Back in the early history of United States, new universities looking for places to call home were called on by towns all over. Take the example of the University of Florida, which could have been located in Ocala, one county away from where it actually is today. Instead, with great incentives from a tiny little railroad town in North Central Florida called Gainesville, UF was located there. Gainesville would most likely still be a tiny rural town, instead of the thriving and growing city it is today, if UF decided to go farther south. So, all local governments know what it means to bring these businesses, sports franchises, etc. to their area: revenue, jobs, and growth.

The job of bringing in these businesses to the community is not IT's. However, we help a great deal by supporting, adding efficiency, and increasing value to government economic development groups. One of the most critical elements to a government, especially local government, is not IT, HR, or Finance. It's not even Police, Fire, or Public Works services. Of course, a community needs those protection services. Likewise, a local government can't run effectively without the support services like HR, IT, and Finance. But, the one critical service that a local government provides may be the most overlooked by citizens: Economic Development, boosting the local economy by creating jobs, bringing in new business, and supporting entrepreneurial start ups. Even crime and homelessness can be linked to economic growth or downturn. You want to reduce crime in a City? It can't be done with law enforcement, alone. Cleaning up neighborhoods and promoting economic growth in an area helps displace crime, too.

Thankfully, governments are trending to these GaaB mentalities once again, at the state and local levels of government, specifically. Local municipalities, county, and even state agencies are realizing, if they want to retain their current populations and grow, they need to promote strong, well planned economic development initiatives and compete in a much smaller, connected world (i.e. a global economy that starts at the local level). Local governments are taking on branding initiatives, marketing campaigns, creating advertising budgets for tourism, and all the other typical activities most people only associate with major corporations, headquartered in shiny New York or Los Angeles high rises.

COMPETITIVE ADVANTAGE

Local governments are beginning to realize that they need to create a competitive advantage in the business of local government. Examples include, lower tax rates, tax incentives, land grants, faster services, digital connectivity, fiber-to-the-home, quality of life, lower cost of living, etc. Of course, there are challenges to this, compounding the inherent challenges of running a government in general. The very nature of government being overly bureaucratic and the rising pressure from constituents to deliver more modern service models, offering more technology-based solutions, increases the gap between innovation and the status quo. It's the same old story of corporate America on the cutting edge and government lagging years, if not decades, behind. The more bureaucracy, the slower the innovation. In theory, some of the bureaucracy is supposed to ensure corruption is prevented; there is fairness for all; and, taxpayers' money is spent wisely. However, high bureaucracy tends to also cause a lot of waste as a natural byproduct of the process. The old maxim that time is money rings true to the private sector, but rarely, if ever, is much thought given to that maxim in the public sector. That's not to say there are not inefficient major private corporations, because there are plenty. It's just that governments tend to not weigh the intangibles they don't know how to measure into their planning equations, more so than the private sector does—a lack of competitive spirit and the right personnel, perhaps.

Ronald Reagan said, *"the best minds are not in government. If any were, business would steal them away."* With the exception of a handful of brilliant people dedicated and drawn to public service—some even coming from the private sector on a mission to improve government—that statement can be true. I have hired my share of brilliant young software engineers and IT professionals over the years. It is tough to attract and retain top-tier personnel, especially in IT, because they know they can take their brilliance out to the private sector and practically write their own paycheck. Those who stay for a while soon realize their fast-moving, innovative minds are quickly hampered by the snail-like pace of government.

Today's workforce, specifically in IT, can't be treated like their parents were. Baby Boomers (1946-1964) were loyal to their organizations and expect the same from younger generations. Gen X'ers (1965-1980) value results, and competence, and are a little less faithful to organizations than their parents were. Gen Y, a.k.a. Millennials (1981-2000), are creative multitaskers, with very little patience, and want the organization to be loyal to them. If not, they move on to another organization. There are actually four generations in the workforce right now. While us Gen X'ers are still prominent in the workforce, Millennials have taken over as the majority.

Large companies in the private sector offer signing bonuses, appropriate base salaries, medical benefits, fringe benefits, and performance bonuses. So, why doesn't the public sector use those tools? "Hey, Brent, because it's the public sector and you can't do that!" No, there are ways you can do that in the public sector, and some local governments are. For example, some agencies offer efficiency bonuses as an incentive to be high-performing and efficient—embrace change and look for waste in the organization. For an employee who changes a process to save money, real tangible money, a percentage of those savings goes to the employee who discovered the waste as a one-time efficiency bonus. And, this works!

Local and state governments are starting to catch up with the private sector. They now see the need to branch out with recruiting efforts, offering higher salaries, with professional development training opportunities (e.g. flextime, telecommuting), and even hiring specialized consultants to train executives and management to build efficient and motivating work environments. This can attract top-tier employees, who can innovate and provide a competitive advantage over other local governments and jurisdictions.

BETTER CUSTOMER SERVICE

Some state and local governments are also realizing to gain and keep a competitive advantage, they need excellent customer service skills to get out of the customer service slump and beat the government stigma (i.e. more attractive for businesses). They are starting to look at taxpayers as actual customers of their products and services. In a government that sees citizens as customers, it is not acceptable to have a staffer of government blow a customer off or have typical government hours of operation, just because citizens don't have a choice. These governments understand, citizens do have a choice, and those choices can positively or negatively affect the communities' quality of life.

Sam Walton, the founder of Wal-Mart, said, "*There is only one boss. The customer. And he can fire everybody in the company from the chairman on down, simply by spending his money somewhere else.*" I think this is also true for citizens of state and local governments. I have heard plenty of stories of people leaving areas because of how sick of the way the state and local government was affecting their family's way of life, especially true among younger generations. This is even more apparent after the 2020 COVID-19 pandemic, where remote working has become a stable norm. Most people can now literally choose what community they want to live in, without worry about a specific job or market. A computer and high-speed internet connection are all you need. Businesses have even moved corporate headquarters, manufacturing facilities, and other operations, for similar reasons. Look at what Elon Musk did, moving from California to Texas, as are many silicon valley businesses. Why? Because, it's more cost-effective and more attractive for business, just like the example of the Braves Baseball franchise moving from Milwaukee to Atlanta. In business terms, they choose to spend their money with a competitor instead. From a business perspective, instead of a Circuit-City customer taking their disposable income to Best Buy or Amazon.com—we know how well that worked out for Circuit-City—we are seeing families and businesses moving to more attractive parts of the country. One family won't have much impact. One big business or major sports franchise could. What about a lot of families? The COVID-19 pandemic showed us that it is very possible to live in one area and work remotely. Someone's job may not even be in the same state, much less the same city as their employer. This could have a daisy chain effect on the local economy, in many ways: Lack of growth in development, dwindling neighborhoods, job scarcity, uptick in crime, etc., but have a great impact on the more desirable communities with lower costs of living (e.g. less crime, less traffic, less stressful life). Declining communities find it hard to recover from such economic change.

Marketing Stunts

The world today is a very different place than it was just twenty years ago. The Millennials and Generation Z are growing up and leaving their hometowns behind, moving to where there are more attractive jobs, companies, entertainment, better governments, and better economies. They don't think twice about picking up and moving away in a small, connected world, where instantaneous communication and technology make working remotely or staying in touch with family and friends easy. State and local governments are starting to realize this and are doing some pretty neat things to attract people and businesses, enticing them to settle down in their area or stay, if it's their hometown. Take Chattanooga, Tennessee, a.k.a the "Gig-City[4]," for example. Chattanooga's municipally owned utility company, the Electric Power Board (EPB) didn't wait around or pull silly stunts, like the 1,095 local municipalities around the US that applied for Google to bring a fiber-optic network and gigabit Internet speeds to their community[5]. The economic benefits are apparent to EPB and the City of Chattanooga, even though selling the internet service and competing with local telecommunications and cable providers came as an afterthought to putting in a smart power grid—If you can call 10,000 Mbs fiber connections to the home vs. 100 to 500 Mbs connections competing. If you think about it, even the local governments who tried to win over Google, were competing against each other. If stunts like jumping into shark tanks aren't a flashy competition, then what would you call it? Did you ever see those weird commercials on TV with a man in a bright yellow suit covered in large question marks or odd stunts and loud attention getting speech performed by local car dealers to attract customers to their dealership? It is the same thing these local governments did. These local governments realized the economic impact and innovation potential of having a fiber-optic network, with gigabit speeds, would mean their economic growth. That realization means they will jump in icy lakes, jump out of airplanes, swim with sharks, change the name of all males in the city to Google Fiber, or just declare the city renamed Google[6] for a month in order to get it. After all, it is human nature.

The City of Chattanooga's Electric Power Board took matters into their own hands, years ahead of anyone else and even before Google Fiber. They built their own full-fledged 900 square-mile fiber-optic network as part of their smart power grid to encompass every home within the service area[7], monitoring the grid, isolating outages, and reducing the time it would take to fix power outages. The result is a gigabit superhighway, providing every home and business in the entirety of Hamilton County, TN, including some surrounding areas, the ability to connect to the internet at the speed of light. That makes for a very attractive location for businesses and tech-savvy citizens to settle down. Since then, several tech companies and citizens coming in for the new jobs created by these businesses have made Chattanooga their new home. It's not over for Chattanooga either. This is just the beginning of their innovation, but this beginning puts them lightyears ahead of their competition—even ahead of Kansas City, MO, where Google choose to put their first fiber network[8].

So, it would seem that governments, at least state and local governments, do indeed compete with each other. And, in some cases, even with other companies, as in the case with local municipalities like Chattanooga and their Electric Power Board that offer high-speed internet access, cable television services in direct competition to that market's cable provider, Comcast.

CREATE COMPETITION AND SHARE THE WEALTH

Some governments share their revenue with business partners to bring good customer service to their constituencies. Here is another example of how having or using GaaB practices through structured competition can increase citizen satisfaction: I restore and work on a lot of cars as a hobby. In June 2013, I bought a vehicle online located in the State of Pennsylvania. When I flew up to take possession of the vehicle, I needed to notarize the title transfer and get a temporary license plate to drive the vehicle the eight hours back to North Carolina, where my wife and I lived at the time.

Being a bit of a car buff, I had done this quite a few times, in many different states, over about a twenty-year period. The most stressful part of the experience is always going to the state DMV. However, this time around, I was pleasantly surprised by PennDOT, the Pennsylvania Commonwealth's Department of Transportation, and their way of handling vehicle registration offices. It was honestly the best DMV experience I have ever had. I was in and out in no time at all. Everyone was super friendly; and, they all seemed to go the extra mile to help customers. I asked the woman who was working with me what the secret was; why were they so efficient? Explaining to her some of the horrors I've seen in state DMVs—looking at you North Carolina!

She explained, Pennsylvania outsources services like vehicle registration to business partners. And, there are a certain number of those outsourced business partners in a given area. In the small town of Doylestown, PA, where I was, there were three such facilities for a population of only about 8,300. In this case, where the facilities were owned by different owners, this meant competition. And, as we know, competition is good for the consumer.

Since the pricing structure was fixed for certain things, the facilities got creative with extras and, most notably, fast customer service. I was inspired and delighted by the whole experience. Even if the pricing structure was to go up for using a system like this, compared to the current method most states use, I bet people would pay a little extra to get in and out quickly, with good customer service. I sure would.

OUTCOMES-BASED BUDGETING

I mentioned outcomes-based budgeting a few times earlier in the book. These types of budgeting practices are starting to take root in public sector agencies across the U.S. It started with the Balanced Scorecard management tool being adopted from the private sector, pushing a performance-based budget along with it—where the budget is driven by specific measures and funded accordingly, instead of the traditional spend it or lose it methods.

Now, state and local governments, like the City of Baltimore, Maryland, the City of Chattanooga, Tennessee, the State of Oregon, City of Richmond, Virginia, City of Lincoln, Nebraska, and many others around the world are using a Budgeting for Outcomes model, or variations thereof. Using budgeting methods like this, the government agencies' financial planning is run more as a business, when performed correctly. There are specific outcomes areas derived from what the citizen base wants and needs. Proposals—business cases and feasibility analysis, as I previously discussed—are submitted by stakeholders and departments within the organization to get projects and departments funded. These proposals are weighed and ranked within the organization's outcomes areas—pillars of excellence for you balanced scorecard users.

Each outcome area is given a specific budgeted amount—a bucket of money, if you will. A line in the budget buckets is drawn. The submitted proposals—offers—are ranked within that outcome. Those ranked above the cutoff get funded; and, the ones below the cutoff do not; at least, that's how it's supposed to work. Essentially, the taxpayers are telling the governments what they are willing to pay for and are expecting results for their investment. What the taxpayers want could become the outcome areas, much the same way a market segment will define the demand for products or services from private sector organizations. It's a fantastic process that I was fortunate enough to be a part of when the City of Chattanooga adopted the approach, under Mayor Andy Berke, when he was first elected back in 2013. These methods allow governments to streamline spending and become much more efficient. Rather than continuing budgets year to year with a spend it or lose it attitude, the governments look to save and be frugal with spending.

CONCLUSION
OPEN MINDED

"It is not necessary to change. Survival is not mandatory." - W. Edwards Deming

Within the IT Group, the CIOs who maintain the status quo or just work to please the boss won't fare well in this new savvy and innovative public sector. The CIO for these governments must add value and have a vision. They must be change agents and innovators. They must be business savvy with significant business and political acumen. They must be a true leader. There is no room in these new public sector agencies for the CIO who runs their IT Group like a Machiavellian dictator. Even before these trends started to become popular in the public sector again, I have always told my staff that those of us living in the area are taxpayers. I want to see my financial investment in the organization and community get used wisely, not wasted frivolously. I challenge my staff to look at what we do in government and our IT group as a business and run it that way.

Not all businesses are run efficiently as they could be. However, there are quite a few best practices that make great companies great. Being an entrepreneur early in life implanted a frugal and efficient tone in me that has never left. As a public sector CIO, you don't have to have this entrepreneurial mindset, but should at the very least be open minded to these concepts. I try to teach this way of thinking to my staff as part of a larger plan to develop future IT leaders. I explain the typical business paradigms related to local government, like how we compete, why we should compete, and how it affects what we do. Then, I challenge them to break the status quo. I teach them to be leaders, innovators, and when they have innovated and business seems to be good, to not be complacent, but instead strive to innovate further. Strive for perfection, even if it can't ever be achieved. To try new things and make mistakes along the way. I teach them to partner with the other areas of the organization and not treat these other departments like customers. Instead, they are partners, all working for the same customer: the taxpayers. I teach them to understand the impact technology has on daily business within the organization, now and in the future.

This is not an easy endeavor for any government CIO to take on. But looking at these practices and the concepts outlined in this book and understanding the purpose and role the CIO should take in this ever-changing industry is a valuable and worthwhile endeavor that will immensely reward you, your staff, your organization, and most importantly your community.

ACKNOWLEDGMENTS

Writing a book is a challenging and rewarding endeavor, one that has been my labor of love for a several years now and I owe a great deal of gratitude to several special people who helped me get here.

I am extremely grateful to my wife, Nicole, and my kids; Lucy, Cullen, Logan, and Evelyn for putting up with long nights of writing, and some weekends with me hunched over a computer screen for hours on end. Thank you all for supporting me and encouraging me to write and see this through, especially to my son Cullen, who has always been my champion; cheering me on at work and with writing this book. His passion and love for helping others may one day lead him to follow a similar path and become a public servant.

I am eternally grateful to Mayor Andy Berke for bringing me to Chattanooga in 2014 and handing me the most challenging and rewarding job of my entire career to that point. Thank you for trusting me with Chattanooga's technology and believing in me to create one of the greatest IT groups in the nation.

A very special thanks to my friend and colleague Jonathan Feldman, who always encouraged me to speak up and push for change when it seemed an impossible task. And a special thanks to Michael Taylor, who sponsored my membership with the Metropolitan Information Exchange (MIX) and introduced me to some of the most brilliant public sector CIOs in the world.

To Shannon Tuffs, thanks for all the starting points for my research and for encouraging me to put all these concepts in writing to share with future public sector CIOs.

To Matt McDarmont, thanks for all the editing sessions, reading, rereading, editing, suggesting, and reediting every single word of this book with me many times over.

And finally, last but certainly not least, to my Dad, my Mom, and my Brother, who are or were public servants and instilled the spark and desire in me to be a public servant.

NOTES

Chapter One

1. Agnew, T. (2012, December 17). 'poor leadership': Report blasts city's it department. Suffolk News-Herald. Retrieved from http://www.suffolknewsherald.com/2012/12/17/poor-leadership-report-blasts-citys-it-department/

2. K. Shaw paper "The value of bosses"; National Boss Poll; APA.org; FSU Boss Study; Shirm; Z.

3. Zenger, J., & Folkman, J. (2014, August 07). Are you sure you're not a bad boss? Retrieved June 10, 2016, from https://hbr.org/2012/08/are-you-sure-youre-not-a-bad-b.

Chapter Two

1. K. Shaw paper "The value of bosses"; National Boss Poll; APA.org; FSU Boss Study; Shirm; Z (Inc.com, Jerk Alert: The Real Costs of Bad Bosses, 2012)

Chapter Eleven

1. Beckett, J. (2000). The "government should run like a business" mantra. American Review of Public Administration, 30(2), 185-204.2. K. Shaw paper "The value of bosses"; National Boss Poll; APA.org; FSU Boss Study; Shirm; Z.

2. Harvey, J. T. (2012, October 10). Why government should not be run like a business. Forbes, Retrieved from http://www.forbes.com/sites/johntharvey/2012/10/05/government-vs-business/.

3. K. Shaw paper "The value of bosses"; National Boss Poll; APA.org; FSU Boss Study; Shirm; Z (Inc.com, Jerk Alert: The Real Costs of Bad Bosses, 2012).

4. Fleming, F. (2001, Feb 15). Milwaukee braves. Retrieved from http://www.sportsecyclopedia.com/nl/milbraves/milbraves.html.

5. Gig city, chattanooga, tn. (n.d.). Retrieved from http://www.thegigcity.com/.

6. Singel, R. (2010, April 08). Hey, google fiber losers: Build it yourselves. WIRED, Retrieved from http://www.wired.com/business/2010/04/google-fiber-losers/.

7. Helft, M. (2010, March 21). Hoping for gift from google? go jump in the lake. The New York Times. Retrieved from http://www.nytimes.com/2010/03/22/technology/22stunts.html.

8. Your gig is here. (n.d.). Retrieved from http://chattanoogagig.com/.

9. Goldman, D. (2011, March 30). Google chooses kansas city for ultra-fast internet. CNN Money, Retrieved from http://money.cnn.com/2011/03/30/technology/google_kansas_city/.

///

INDEX

ABOUT THE AUTHOR

Brent Messer is an award-winning thought leader, author, and international speaker on the world of IoT, Smart Cities, Agile, digital transformation, and innovation; named to State Scoop's Golden Gov: City Executive of the Year in 2020. Brent has worked in Information Technology since 1997 and spent eight years as CIO for the City of Chattanooga, transforming the City into an agile and innovative civic tech powerhouse. Recognized the world over as one of the most innovative cities in the United States and known as the "Gig City" for their 10-gigabit municipally-owned broadband network.

CPSIA information can be obtained
at www.ICGtesting.com
Printed in the USA
LVHW110524150622
721142LV00004B/5/J